Honoring Motherhood

Another SkyLight Paths Book
Edited by Lynn L. Caruso

*Blessing the Animals: Prayers and Ceremonies
to Celebrate God's Creatures, Wild and Tame*

Honoring Motherhood

Prayers, Ceremonies & Blessings

Edited and with Introductions by

Lynn L. Caruso

Walking Together, Finding the Way®
SKYLIGHT PATHS®
PUBLISHING
Woodstock, Vermont

Honoring Motherhood:
Prayers, Ceremonies & Blessings

2008 First Printing
© 2008 by Lynn L. Caruso

See pp. 234–41 for a continuation of this copyright page.

Library of Congress Cataloging-in-Publication Data
Available upon request.

10 9 8 7 6 5 4 3 2 1

Manufactured in the United States of America
❀ Printed on Recycled Paper
Jacket Design: Jenny Buono
Illustrations: Jenny Buono
SkyLight Paths, "Walking Together, Finding the Way," and colophon are trademarks of LongHill Partners, Inc., registered in the U.S. Patent and Trademark Office.

SkyLight Paths Publishing is creating a place where people of different spiritual traditions come together for challenge and inspiration, a place where we can help each other understand the mystery that lies at the heart of our existence.

SkyLight Paths sees both believers and seekers as a community that increasingly transcends traditional boundaries of religion and denomination—people wanting to learn from each other, *walking together, finding the way.*

Walking Together, Finding the Way
Published by SkyLight Paths Publishing
A Division of Longhill Partners, Inc.
Sunset Farm Offices, Route 4, P.O. Box 237
Woodstock, VT 05091
Tel: (802) 457-4000   Fax: (802) 457-4004
www.skylightpaths.com

For my mother, Doris K. Liebert

"The pure love which [your children] express
is seldom put in words, nor could it be.
Their love is their very life. You made them
and you make them daily."

Donald H. Liebert

Editor's Note: This excerpt is from a letter found in my mother's hope chest. The lines were written by my father nearly forty years ago.

Contents

Introduction

In the days preceding the birth of my first son, I often walked to a small brook at the end of our road. As the song thrush returned to the riverbank and the sugar maple slowly loosened her grip on winter—uncurling her leaves like small green fists—I found parallels between my own experience and the world outside my window. As Kahlil Gibran wrote, "Everything in nature bespeaks the mother.... This earth is the mother of trees and flowers. It produces them, nurses them, and weans them."

My child's first sunset was the last day of winter, his first sunrise—curled beside me—the start of spring and the dawn of a new season for both of us. This sacred moment stands at the heart of *Honoring Motherhood*. A moment linking me to the eternal chain of life, like generations of women before me. Now, as the mother of three, I have found *that* moment to be the first of many. Like nature's seasons, motherhood is constantly evolving. There is a season for mistakes and for repair. For letting the field lie fallow and for new birth.

Honoring Motherhood begins with our maternal ancestors who tilled the soil before us and influence us as women and mothers today. Using the metaphor of the planting seasons, the book follows the stages of the mother-child relationship, from awaiting a child's arrival, through years of change, growth, and even loss. The collection offers original multifaith ceremonies for new motherhood, as well as an exploration of the Maternal Divine in various faith traditions. The book concludes with a look at the implications of sowing the seeds of love gained through motherhood out into the greater world.

Honoring Motherhood is for all mothers: traditional, single, adoptive, foster, step, and bereaved. The writers, from many faith traditions and backgrounds, honor their mothers and their own personal experience of motherhood. Within these pages, motherhood is portrayed as a complex experience—often bittersweet and sometimes ripe with paradox—a journey that is at once beautiful and unsettling, a great joy and a vessel for sorrow, an inheritance and at times a loss.

The cherry blossom that graces the cover of this book is revered in Japan for its beauty and its transience. Its flowers are exquisite, yet the petals fall at their peak, and both qualities add to the beauty and complexity of this flower. Such "letting go is something we can't escape as mothers," writes Kathleen Finley. "Our children start leaving us from the moment they're born." Yet in the end, the cherry is one of nature's sweetest fruits.

A mother gives of her very body, offering her womb to carry and her breasts to nourish. Even her arms, Maya Angelou writes, were "molded / Into a cradle to hold me." Motherhood is both exhilarating and depleting, and it changes our lives, often with very little return. Just as the gardener waters, nourishes, and tends the cherry seedling, so too will there be times, as a mother, when you are the one doing all the giving, and there will be sacred moments when you receive.

The writers in *Honoring Motherhood* affirm that other mothers and our creator God walk beside us in each season. They acknowledge that the work mothers do is quiet and often unrecognized but ultimately profound and life-changing, and it touches the world. Whether you are opening this book in the early spring light of new motherhood or reading it in a quiet room with your children grown, there is something here for you. These are not words of advice, but of honor. May they replenish a bit of what you give away every day.

1

Tilling the Soil
Honoring Our Maternal Ancestors

"Tilling the Soil" invites us to explore our maternal ancestors who prepared the earth before us—ancestors who shape who we are as women and as mothers. My own childhood is filled with memories of canning jars of applesauce with my German grandmother, and of camping on the banks of the Yukon River with my mother. Even though the tart taste of the apples and the sound of the thundering river have faded, the memories of these strong women—their patience, love, secrets, and adventure—remain. As DeLona Campos-Davis writes of her own mother, "I find traces of you in my mothering."

Many of the pieces in this section are powerful stories that have been passed down for generations. Jeanne Murray Walker retraces the steps of her

1

grandmother's arrival at Ellis Island, and Claire
Rudolf Murphy describes her strong ancestors who
survived the Great Hunger. Upon her mother's death,
Gunilla Norris reflects on the life they shared, describ-
ing the act of remembering her mother as the "composting of memory." Over time, she writes, these
layers of memories turn "to soil in one's being."

The richest compost includes varied scraps of
material—brilliant sugar maple leaves mixed in with
rotten apple skins—and it is the same with our maternal inheritance. There are parts we cherish and parts
we wish to forget. For many, the memories of maternal
ancestors are primarily stories of love and strength.
But for others, maternal lineage is not an inheritance
worth celebrating, and they may worry that what was
lacking could hurt their own mothering. In reflecting
on our maternal lineage, we identify what bears pass-
ing on to future generations and what is best to let go
of, hoping not to repeat the hurtful parts of the past.

Maude Meehan likens studying her mother's
hands to studying a map of the land, hoping to gain a
glimpse of the past and direction for the future: "I ...
trace with my aging hands / seamed furrows of my
mother land / Explore the future." We have all inherited
a motherland from those who have preceded us. For
good or bad, rich or barren, it is the ground in which
we are planted. Tilling the soil is hard work, but ultimately reworking our own soil will make us healthier
mothers.

Many societies recognize the importance of raising children in a supportive community of loving caregivers who will remind each generation of the ground on which they stand. Theirs is a soil tilled by both kin and community. The Navajo consider all people of the mother's clan to be "my mother," and many indigenous societies use the term *Grandmother* to address all elder women. As Jan Reynolds writes, "If mother is the heart of the continuum, grandmother is the soul."

The autumn before my sons' great-grandmother died, she gave me dahlia tubers to plant in our spring garden. I wrapped them in a brown paper bag and stored them in my basement through that cold Northwest winter. But Margaret never lived to show me how to plant them in the spring. She gave me the potential to grow something beautiful, but left much for me to learn. As mothers, we have been handed the seeds. Through generations the soil has been tilled by the hands of mothers and grandmothers before us. Our work is to take what we are given and make it bloom, to plant our children firmly in this sacred ground.

One generation plants the trees
another gets the shade.

Chinese proverb

∾

We give thanks for our maternal ancestors.
For those we never knew but who return to us
    in the faces of our sons and daughters.
For ancestors, with their strengths and frailties,
    who make us who we are.
For women who walked before us
    and worked the soil of our very lives.
For those who planted seeds,
    knowing the shade
    was for their children's children.
May we pass on to future generations
    the hope and promise revealed in their lives.

Lynn L. Caruso

∾

We find ourselves in a world that is already
planted but is also still being planted as at first.

Henry David Thoreau, The Dispersion of Seeds

Reflecting on the old quince tree in her yard:

Its dark shape in the middle of a very green lawn seems appropriate. A great-great-grandmother tree that is still bearing fruit.

I observe Mother's Day with this old tree. I cannot call my mother anymore. I miss that very much. I cannot call my grandmother. I am the grandmother now and I do not know how to really be that. Not yet, anyway. So I stand here in the garden and try to feel the old tree.

I want to learn from it. One thing I have understood is that I can bear fruit even into the later years of my life. I see that in the tree. It also tells me of the power of roots. This tree would not be standing now without some wonderful taproot holding it in place. I want to believe that I am growing a root like that into the ground of my being.

Gunilla Norris, Journeying in Place

~

These women are the link between what was and what is now. If mother is the heart of the continuum, grandmother is the soul.

Jan Reynolds, Mother and Child

THE SHAWL

Somewhere on Ellis Island
my mother's mother lost the shawl
the women of the town crocheted for her
out of mauves and purples,
old tunes twisted in the strands,
and clever plots
woven, woven in the pattern.
It was a gift.

Away from that shawl
my mother's mother had to move,
toward the waiting train, toward Minnesota,
through the smell of gasoline,
through the sycamores
whose leaves clinked down
like foreign coins.
She tripped over
a broken step, caught herself,

steadied her canvas bag, paid
her money, wrote her name on the form, washed
in communal showers, put on
her skirt with its stubborn hem. When
they opened the wire gate, she bowed
and hoisted the bag higher
to step over the threshold
into the calling distance
where the years stretched out
plain as good dirt

and she began to imagine
the calamity and extreme grace
of someone wearing that mauve shawl
till every night in dreams
she chopped it,
burned it, and
when it rose again,
she buried it.

She spent every minute
chasing the furious rooster, dropping
report cards into her apron pocket, bargaining
in zero weather,
forgetting that old grace,
finally carrying
her children's
children on her hip,
while she stirred the soup,

their breath soft as moss,
their tiny feet
stuttering against her.
My feet, my breath.
She bore my mother
like a speck toward me
as I bear you
in this plain dress
towards your own children,
holding in my empty hands
her glorious shawl,
sunrise over Ellis Island.

Jeanne Murray Walker

I DREAM OF MY GRANDMOTHER
AND GREAT GRANDMOTHER

I imagine them walking down rocky paths
toward me, strong, Italian women returning
at dusk from fields where they worked all day
on farms built like steps up the sides
of steep mountains, graceful women carrying water
in terra cotta jugs on their heads.

What I know of these women, whom I never met,
I know from my mother, a few pictures
of my grandmother, standing at the doorway
of the fieldstone house in Santo Mauro,
the stories my mother told of them,

but I know them most of all from watching
my mother, her strong arms lifting sheets
out of the cold water in the wringer washer,
or from the way she stepped back,
wiping her hands on her homemade floursack apron,
and admired her jars of canned peaches
that glowed like amber in the dim cellar light.

I see those women in my mother
as she worked, grinning and happy,
in her garden that spilled its bounty
        into her arms.
She gave away baskets of peppers,
lettuce, eggplant, gave away bowls of pasta,

meatballs, zeppoli, loaves of homemade bread.
"It was a miracle," she said.
"The more I gave away, the more I had to give."

Now I see her in my daughter,
the same unending energy,
that quick mind,
that hand, open and extended to the world.
When I watch my daughter clean the kitchen counter,
watch her turn, laughing,

I remember my mother as she lay dying,
how she said of my daughter, "that Jennifer,
she's all the treasure you'll ever need."

I turn now, as my daughter turns,
and see my mother walking toward us
down crooked mountain paths,
behind her, all those women
dressed in black.

Maria Mazziotti Gillan

~

Understanding the Divine flow of life makes sense of
the sacrifice of mothering. I pass on to my child the
best of what I have. I stand on the shoulders of my
ancestors, each generation, hopefully, extending the
reach of the previous one.... This is evolution.

Jacqueline Kramer, Buddha Mom

COMMUNION

For Grandmother Margaret

Stepping stone on stone
through her garden's gate, Margaret
finds us with her promises to spray
for worms in the fall, her fingers
thimbling deep into the wine of cherries
in the bowl she's brought to share, her silver
hair stitched with coral shells from the chestnut
tree, while my son nurses curled at my
breast, in one mystic inhale of *take,*
eat and do this in remembrance
of the afternoon beneath the lyric
blossoms of the chestnut tree where bees
drink their own sweet nectar from the stamen's
cup, and my son, this child who's seen
the underside of me, like a moonflower
knowing all there is to know of night,
fingers out with hands like startled stars,
to touch the ruby stain in his great
grandmother's palm, still clinging
to the cream of my body with his soft
mouth, and in this giving
and receiving, there is water
into wine.

Lynn L. Caruso

CARTOGRAPHER

I stroke her papery skin
now lined, worn tissue thin
as ancient maps
Trace with my aging hands
seamed furrows of my mother land
Explore the future

Maude Meehan

~

CONTINUUM

Almost a year has passed
since you let go of life.
Spring comes.
Outside the window
small migrant birds
move delicate as grace notes
on the wire. I watch a sparrow
pull dead twigs from the porch vine
to weave into its nest below the eaves.
A daughter's belly swells,
a grandchild moves toward life,
and you are present for me
in this promise, in these affirmations.

Maude Meehan

I WOULD NOT BE HERE

I would not be here,
if Great-great grandmother Mooney from Cork
had not married a Huddy from Clare,
and escaped famine's death grip.

Landing in New Orleans,
she birthed a daughter, traveling
to Iowa by covered wagon.

So tiny she fit into a cigar box,
little Annie E. should have died,
from her mum's lack of food and care
on the coffin ship crossing the Atlantic.

But Grandma Huddy would not let
blackened potatoes and British landlords
take her baby girl, too.

Our matriarch smoked a clay pipe,
and never learned to read,
but in one generation changed it all.
With grit and rosary beads,
she buried the Great Hunger,
made certain Annie E. attended school.

Annie E.'s daughter Rose carried on.
Pillar of church and community,
Daughters, college graduates, all four.

My mother Frances Collins,
born during one war,
married in the second,
raised us with a Catholic faith,
so bedrock deep it couldn't be cracked.

Determined to get ahead,
these women never looked back.
"Not flower people, not a one."
Irish orchids and yarrow,
already steeped in our pores.

Five generations later, my daughter returned.
On Irish sod and Celtic rock, she discovered
the love and strength
that rooted Grandma Huddy
sustains her now.

Claire Rudolf Murphy

ANCESTORS

My ancestors grew potatoes, rye and oats,
in the sandy soil of the Baltic Coast,
went to the sea and pulled in nets
with struggling fish unto the beach,
fish that were later smoked in the smokehouse
or fried and served with boiled potatoes for
    supper.

This is the land where in springtime
yellow buttercups bloomed in vernal pools
and bluebells on higher ground,
where the cuckoo called me from the birch forest
and the stork blessed the house
where my grandparents lived.

This is where my mother Karline was born
at sunrise on Easter Sunday
when Latvia was still a province
of Russia. My grandparents were first cousins.
here is where I first encountered sorrow
in my grandmother Sophie's voice.

With a black scarf on her widowed head
she scurried about, like a crow
in a barren field, raking in hay,
milking cows, counting chickens and eggs.

Here in 1919, on the night of August 9
a farmhand killed my grandfather,
his niece and nephew.
Unarmed, with a small child at her side
Sophie faced the killer and stared him down.

Further back my ancestors were serfs
and labored for czars and German landlords.
They are said to have lightened their burdens by
placing the old and the weak on sleds
and bringing them to the forest
in the winter to watch the snow fall.

During World War II when the rest of us
fled to safer lands we left Sophie behind
on the farm. Now I carry her.

Sibilla Hershey

~

When we touch the present moment deeply, we
also touch the past ... we have to let the ancestors
in us be liberated. The moment that we can offer
them joy, peace, and freedom, we offer joy,
peace, and freedom to ourselves, our children,
and their children at the same time.

Thich Nhat Hanh, Teachings on Love

HABAÑERA

We dismantle her
house, divide the things
we've lived among, the books
and photographs, lift Chagall's
"Musician" off its hook, unplug
the stereo, collect librettos,
1936, Caruso at the Met.

Small things speak up
emptying
her boxes full of pills
the special phone
with giant numerals, its shrill
ring, two hearing aids,
her teeth, the upper partial
resting in a blue plastic case.

We dismantle the bed
remove the rail, the kind
you use to keep a child
from falling in the night,
find her glasses folded
on the table. She always left
them open, ready, ear pieces
jutting from the frame —

Yellow jonquils glow
before the mantel mirror.
Her friend Minna brought them,
knowing it would change nothing,
mother, singing behind the rhythm
of a Carmen aria, becoming eggshell,
loose in her big chair, no longer knowing
Minna but loving Carmen, loving yellow.

Edythe Haendel Schwartz

~

[When someone we love dies] the composting of memory begins — the mystery of the years, layers and layers of shared life turning to soil in one's being.... Through the seasons my memories are composted, too, and like the leaves they come together. Turned over and over, in time they finally turn into something new — rich, dark earth in the palm of my hand.

Gunilla Norris, Journeying in Place

MY SCRIPTURAL MOTHERS

Thank you,

Eve, for loving Adam, the father of your children.

Hagar, for your bravery in the desert. You kept Ishmael alive with the waters of Zam Zam.

Shiphrah, for ignoring Pharaoh's edict and saving the life of a Hebrew baby boy, at risk of your own. You inspire me to help protect children today.

Thank you,

Miriam, for mothering a new nation. You moved through anger at God and your brothers Moses and Aaron, into joy, singing and dancing with the women of Israel.

Ruth and Naomi, for honoring each other as mother and daughter, instead of bickering in-laws. Together you found new life after tragic loss.

Hannah, for showing me how to let go of bitterness born of barrenness, by celebrating the birth of your long awaited Samuel, and later letting him go to do God's work.

Thank you,

Abigail, for stopping the senseless fighting between David and your foolish husband Nabal with your gift of negotiation.

Esther, for your fearless defense of your Jewish
   birthright at risk of death. You reveal that
   beauty is not just skin deep, but comes from
   the deepest part of a woman's soul.

Mary, mother of Jesus, for your friendship with
   your cousin Elizabeth during your time of
   uncertainty and joy. You remind me to
   appreciate the blessings of sisters and friends.

Thank you,

Syrophonecian Woman, for demanding that
   attention be paid to your suffering daughter.
   You spoke out and Jesus listened.

Mary Magdalene, for standing by the tomb when
   everyone else ran in fear.

Lydia, for mothering a new church alongside
   Paul. The services held in your home in
   Philippi reveal that women have not always
   stood in the shadows of the church.

Mother of James and John, for your humanness in
   petitioning Jesus for the welfare of your sons.
   You reveal that even two thousand years ago,
   our greatest challenge as mothers is to let go
   of pride and anxiety for our children, and
   drink of our own cup.

Thank you, *Scriptural Mothers*, for showing me how to
   speak out, let go, stand firm, be present,
   be brave.

Claire Rudolf Murphy

PLANTED IN HOLY GROUND

Planted in holy ground.
Childhood rich with blessing
And manure.
Mother, through a glass darkly
Pitching from a fork
Feeding with a spoon
Heaviness falls as warmth.
Either germinates.

Planted in holy ground.
Mothered through generations
Of drought.
Tilled. Watered.
Composted. I bear rosy fruit
Tastes bitter.
Nibbles at my core.

Planted in holy ground.
Branches reach with buds.
Sap flows.
Leaves curl inward.
I yank on my roots.
Moan through fall, winter.

Planted in holy ground.
No force stronger
Than spring sprouting.
If I allow it
From the earth
With the sun.
In mystery. Abundance.

M. F.

~

I find traces of you in my mothering. Knowing all the words to all the songs of *The Sound of Music*. Playing "Come to me, Come" in the car. Tripling the cookie recipe, from the measurements written in the margins of your recipe book. I'd rather you were here to do these things. Your sisters and friends gather pieces of you and share them back with me. And I am grateful.

I know you wouldn't be a saint. I'm sure you'd drive me crazy sometimes. We'd take each other for granted, and maybe forget to call enough. But the glimpses I have of you as a woman, not just my mom, make me think you'd be doing adventurous and courageous things. And I would be proud.

I imagine knowing you as a friend, seeing you as a grandma, still having you here.

DeLona Campos-Davis

FIRST LESSONS

Through the rainy streets of Paris
Madeline is hurried to hospital.

Under the garden fence, Peter Rabbit
scurries from the farmer's savage hoe,

while on Africa's hot plains
Babar's kin are chased and captured.

In my mother's lap I heard
first stories of this world's suffering

in that music pouring
from her throat as she read.

Against the pulse beat of my mother's heart,
close in the crook of her arm,

I inhaled a sweet pungency:
memory of milk and the sunned

warmth of skin — my earliest
fisthold of earth.

And curled against her
on the rust-colored couch,

turning the pages, I learned
beneath each of our stories

beats the great love
of the earth-body
warming us.

Alicia Hokanson

~

The journey toward motherhood for any woman begins with conception. But whose? Did my maternal path begin when my first child was conceived? The casual answer to that question is yes. But the true answer, I think, is that the journey began long ago, with my conception, or my mother's, or her mother's or even further back in the chain of mothers before us. For me, as for every woman, all the incidents of my life, all that makes up my character and personality, my DNA, what I read and experience, where I've traveled from and to, all of it led me to motherhood. And all of it affects how I mother. Nothing, however, exerts an influence on how a woman raises a child as powerfully as does her own mother.

Kathryn Black, Mothering without a Map

TELL ME, MOTHER

Mother, tell me everything you know from your old sorrows. Tell me how he is born and how his tiny body comes to be, bound with the core of my body.

Tell me if he'll search for my breast by himself, or if I should offer it, encouraging him.

Give me your knowledge of love now, mother. Teach me the new caresses, delicate, more delicate than those of a spouse.

How will I wash his little head in the days to come? And how will I wrap him up so I won't harm him?

Teach me, mother, that lullaby you rocked me with. That one will make him sleep better than any other songs.

Gabriela Mistral

~

We think back through our mothers
if we are women.

Virginia Woolf, A Room of One's Own

PIANO

Softly, in the dusk, a woman is singing to me;
Taking me back down the vista of years, till I see
A child sitting under the piano,
    in the boom of the tingling strings
And pressing the small, poised feet
    of a mother who smiles as she sings.

In spite of myself, the insidious mastery of song
Betrays me back, till the heart of me
    weeps to belong
To the old Sunday evenings at home,
    with winter outside
And hymns in the cozy parlor,
    the tinkling piano our guide.

So now it is vain for the singer to burst
    into clamor
With the great black piano appassionato.
    The glamour
Of childish days is upon me,
    my manhood is cast
Down in the flood of remembrance,
    I weep like a child for the past.

D. H. Lawrence

Thou art thy mother's glass, and she in thee
Calls back the lovely April of her prime.

William Shakespeare, "Sonnet III"

~

I AM A GROWNUP

Now that I look more like my mother
Than myself.

Now that I have rocked her
And comforted her
Smelling her familiar hair
Telling her it was all right
Knowing it wasn't.

Now when I move through
The silent neighborhood at night
I am not gliding home on my bike.
And the smell of somebody's evening meal
Rolled like a warm carpet to the street
Is not for me.

Lauri Hewitt

Mother God, Creator, Wisdom,
Thank you for the mother who gave me life.
Thank you for her imperfect love.
Where she faltered, give me direction.
Where she neglected, help me grow.
Where she wounded, heal me.
Lead me into the womb.
I choose the pain of rebirth.
Bitter grief dissolves.
Waters flowing freedom and forgiveness.
Wail bringing release.
Breast offering life.
Joy and pain.
Milk for mother and child.
Thank you, Mother
For pouring your life.
Blessing me.

M. F.

~

I forgive my Ancestors for any negative actions
that affect my life and make it harder for me to
live in the freedom of a child of God. I release
them from bondage and judgments and make
peace with them today, in Jesus' name.

Fr. Robert DeGrandis,
The Ten Commandments of Prayer

During an exasperating trip to the grocery store
with her elderly mother:

I prayed to see her through God's eyes, but nothing happened. It was too much of a stretch. So I prayed to see her through the eyes of a friend, the eyes of someone just watching the movie of my mother shopping. And I got to see this short sweet woman with a badly pleated memory, working hard to keep herself in independent living. I saw an elderly English woman cadging coupons so she could pay her own way and not have to ask her skittish children for help. And then this woman popped back out of the waves right beside me in line, goggle-eyed, blinky, and I know this is not clinically a miracle, but it felt like one, because I finally started laughing. So maybe not a miracle, but grace. Grace means you go from slavery to freedom, freedom from the bondage of self—from small and in a hurry, tapping your foot with impatience, to holding your mother's warm hand.

Anne Lamott, "The Things We Carry"

2

Spring
A Season of Planting and New Life

*T*he birth of my first child coincided with the return of starlings to my feeder and the bloom of magnolias along our quiet Princeton Street. Spring is the season when everything is seeking to be born — to live. The natural world begins anew each spring, and it is in this season of beginnings that the material in this section is grounded. These writers describe the months preceding a child's arrival as a time of great hope and anticipation, whether it be the sacred experience of pregnancy, birth, and the first days of life with a new child, or the expectancy and joyous arrival of an adopted child.

My good friends had waited nearly a year to bring their adopted son home from India. In our conversations, my friend's anguish was palpable as she confided,

"I just want to hold my baby." This sentiment, shared by expectant mothers everywhere, was magnified by the fact that her son was beginning life in another's arms.

During pregnancy, the mother's life as she knows it is transformed. Her attention is drawn inward to her developing child, and, as many mothers do, she may experience a heightened sense of spiritual awareness. In the miracle of pregnancy and birth, mother and child share one body, and there is great spiritual significance in this first sacrificial act of communion: the exchange of breath, blood, and nourishment. In Asia, pregnancy itself is viewed as a spiritual practice that has precedence over all other practices for the entire nine months. Pregnant women are encouraged to spend time in prayer and contemplation.

As Jewish philosopher Martin Buber reflected, infants dwell in the womb of their mothers but also "in the womb of the great mother." Pregnancy is a time of conception for both the mother and the child. Our child is becoming a self, and we are becoming a new self. As Margaret Anne Huffman writes, her unborn child was "growing a new me: her mother."

At the time of delivery both mother and child leave things behind to enter a new season of life—the child leaves the safety and comfort of the womb; the mother leaves the security and familiarity of her old life. And it is in this newness that mother and child meet. In those first days after the infant leaves the known universe of the womb, the mother's body continues to be the child's environment. We soothe our infants with our heartbeat, warm their tiny bodies with our own body heat, nourish and rock these little ones in our arms. With my firstborn, I remember the amazing initial realization that I was everything he needed, that he was formed and nurtured in my womb, and with my body I kept him alive.

In this "Spring" section, mothers recall those first sacred moments of connection. Margaret Anne Huffman describes her feelings when she first held her adopted daughter as a "wondrous greening of my soul." But even from these first intimate days, we experience the paradoxes of motherhood. There are the moments of "delight," as Janeen Steer writes of her son Asher. There are also the doubts, such as those Lauren McFeaters describes in her painful struggle with postpartum depression: "This privilege of parenthood is a haunting."

Many of the writers in this section portray mother as the first love, the source of all love. Reflecting on her work with Hindu women, Sister Nivedita states that when a woman gives birth, "the whole world recognizes that henceforth there will be one soul at least to whom her every act is holy."

This may seem like a daunting responsibility. How could we, in our depleted state, be the embodiment of holiness and love? How can we even rise once more in the night to our child's cries? But, as Margaret Hebblethwaite reflects while cradling her child, we can turn to God for sustenance, the divine source of motherly love: "I'm holding you," she writes, "and God's holding me."

BLESSING FOR EXPECTANT MOTHERS

Remember always, your body is sacred ground.
Your roots are strong and the sun holy.
The gardeners who came before—
mother, grandmother, great-grandmother—
tilled your soil with the compost of their lives.

And now, you hold the seeds.
Plant them deeply in the furrow of this land.

May what comes to you as flower
one day ripen into fruit.
And in your final years,
may they return as shade.

Lynn L. Caruso

~

The seed is within the banyan tree, and within
the seed are the flowers, the fruits, and the shade.

Kabir, fifteenth-century mystic poet of India

It is true
I was created in you.
It is also true
That you were created for me.
I owned your voice.
It was shaped and turned to soothe me.
Your arms were molded
Into a cradle to hold me, to rock me.
The scent of your body was the air
Perfumed for me to breathe.

Maya Angelou

~

A mother lovingly nourishes the son who has entered her womb, and brings him forth with care.

Buddhist saying

~

The Lord your God will maintain with you the covenant loyalty that he swore to your ancestors; he will love you, bless you, and multiply you; he will bless the fruit of your womb and the fruit of your ground.

Deuteronomy 7:12–13

For it was you who formed my inward parts;
you knit me together in my mother's womb.
I praise you, for I am fearfully and wonderfully
    made.
Wonderful are your works; that I know very well.
My frame was not hidden from you,
when I was being made in secret,
intricately woven in the depths of the earth.
Your eyes beheld my unformed substance.
In your book were written
all the days that were formed for me,
when none of them as yet existed.

Psalm 139:13–16

~

He makes you,
In the wombs
Of your mothers,
In stages, one after another,
In three veils of darkness.
Such is Allah, your Lord
And Cherisher.

Qur'an 39:7

EARTH'S IMAGE

I hadn't seen the true image of the Earth before. The Earth has the shape of a woman with a child in her arms (with her young in her wide arms).

I'm beginning to recognize the maternal feeling of things. The mountain that watches me is also mother, and in the afternoon the fog plays like a child on her shoulders and knees.

Now I remember a gorge in the valley. A stream went singing through its deep bed, completely hidden by the craggy ground covered with brambles. Now I'm like the gorge; I feel this small arroyo sing in my depths and I have given him my flesh for a cover of brambles until he comes up to the light.

Gabriela Mistral

DANCING PARTNERS

I dance in a cumbersome,
out-sized waltz of new life
in love with my body
as it blooms and hovers
over the tiny being
cradled near my heart
as if already on my lap.
I savor outlandish cravings,
rehearsals for a lifetime of yearnings
on behalf of this becoming-daughter.
Naked in morning sunlight,
I anoint my roundness with oil,
lullabying its nestling, who, in
matching conception and gestation
is growing a new me: her mother.

Margaret Anne Huffman

~

I am a woman giving birth to myself.

Anonymous

DEAR GOD, BLESS ALL MOTHERS ...
especially expectant mothers

In this intense nine months, when mothers-to-be are realizing that their life is about to change forever, bless them God, because they feel alternately elated and alarmed. Help each mother-in-waiting to understand that she has been carefully chosen, by both you and by her baby, to guide it through its early years on planet Earth. Let her know that she will never be alone in the process. Help her to remember that her baby is your own perfect creation, just as she, herself, is your own perfect creation. Thank you God, for making each of your creations uniquely perfect in its own way. Amen.

Lauren McLaughlin

~

May every living being ...
those already born,
those waiting to be born,
May all attain peace.

Attributed to The Sutta-Nipâta

PRAYER FOR A DIFFICULT PREGNANCY

"Those who wait for the Lord shall renew their
    strength."

(Isaiah 40:31)

Creator God,
Comfort the mother who waits anxiously
for her baby's arrival.
Through her challenging pregnancy bring peace.
Help her to relinquish control,
trusting that you formed this child within her womb
and will watch over this little one until birth —
    and beyond.
Renew her strength for the days ahead.
And in your perfect timing,
deliver this child safely into her waiting arms.
Amen.

Lynn L. Caruso

~

To the mother alone
it has been given, that her soul
during the nine months should
touch the soul of the child.

Jean Baptiste Lacordaire

BLESSING FOR A SINGLE MOTHER

God, who knows the future of us all,
bless this woman as she faces
the prospect of motherhood alone.
Give her all the graces and wisdom she will need
to make good choices for her child and for her
   own life.
Help her to weigh the prospect of adoption,
if that is appropriate.
And help her to know the support and care
she has from others,
as well as your deep love.
Give her the strength and courage
to love this child well;
hold her close to you and wrap her in your love.
Amen.

Kathleen Finley

*Note: If this blessing is done by someone other than the mother, that
person should place a hand on the mother. If she is saying this prayer
alone, she should pray with her hands open before her and change the
wording as needed.*

BLESS THIS BELLY

Bless this belly
    expanding, stretching, alarmingly large
Bless these thighs
    strong, squatting
Bless these hips
    widening, opening
Bless these breasts
    nourishing, comforting
Bless these arms
    holding, safe
Bless this body
    forever marked, changed
Never the same,
    for having co-created with God.

DeLona Campos-Davis

BLESSING

May pain be far away from you,
May fear be far away from you,
May there be cool rain without storm.
By the Lord of life, may you be blessed.
By the Lord of life, may your child be blessed.

Hindu prayer, adapted by Lynn L. Caruso

~

INVOCATION

May this woman give birth happily!
May she give birth,
May she stay alive,
May she walk in health before
thy divinity!
May she give birth happily
and worship thee!

*Mesopotamian invocation to Ishtar,
the Goddess of Morning*

BIRTH

Old things are passed away.
Behold, all things are become new

For Wendy Weger

I watch the midwife pull the white paper down.
She rips the old part off, pats the table,
says, "Climb up here. Use the stirrups."

Granite shifts along a fault, striking sparks.
"Is this comfortable?" she asks.
I gasp and breathe, hout, hout hout,

while she unpacks chrome instruments.
She tilts the spotlight down,
trains its glare to the perineum.

The contraction grinds our muscles
on each other, tearing continents apart.
your skull scrapes my backbone till

Lightning torches all our ribs.
I search the earth for a way out of this.
But we are the earth. The earth fractures itself.

"Relax," the midwife says in another language.
The membrane breaks, weeping light and water.
You ride water downstream, towards the falls and

"Push!" she says. Light pours over the edge,
floods the table, stuns the midwife's
knotty hands. In one minute,

a new order, a new earth, transforming
old orthodoxies, transfiguring the room.
In the end, we are faithful

to what cannot be avoided.
Light breaks from your new knees
and shoulders. Light peals
like an unbearable, high bell.

Jeanne Murray Walker

~

SONG OF A WOMAN IN LABOR

towering rocks
sound
in the evening
with them
I cry

Papago, North American Indian

MAEVE

Out you came from that dark,
wet space you shared

with your brother. Where
for months you thrived,

tucked in the lower, left
quadrant of my womb.

Twin A, they labeled you
though your name would be

a Celtic goddess from
an eternal world; a queen

who chose and won her battles,
outlived her mates.

When your brother pushed
and scrunched — head down, nose

to the rear — so he'd meet me
first, you were left to ride

the amniotic waves alone.
And didn't you swallow some

and inhale others — coming
into this world needing

an oxygen tube. But who's
to say bottled air saved you,
and not spirit passed on in a name?

Meghan Nuttall Sayres

~

Spirit enters flesh
And for all it's worth
Charges into earth
In birth after birth
Ever fresh and fresh.

Robert Frost, excerpt from
"Kitty Hawk"

~

We have enjoined on man
Kindness to his parents:
In pain did his mother
Bear him, and in pain
Did she give him birth.

Qur'an 46:15

POND

For Isaac, born the last day of winter

Spring arrives.
The pond turns over in the cool wind.
The surface I have come to know so well—
where small loons overwinter and water-striders
skate across the glass—
becomes the ground.
All things hidden in the black silt,
all things forgotten or never known,
rise to the surface,
become the new pond.
Cool water that could fill a stone pitcher,
a glass vase, a life.

My child arrives.
The pond turns over in the cool wind.
The surface I have come to know —
a quiet house and time enough to write,
weekends on the train to the city —
sink to the bottom.
The water stirs, my son crowns,
rings echo from his first breath.
And from the cup of his hands, I drink.
New water that could fill
my life.

Lynn L. Caruso

Note: In spring, ponds are stratified with a warm surface area and
cooler bottom layer. In the presence of cold wind or rain, these two layers can be rapidly mixed, leading to the phenomenon that is known as
the pond "turning over."

To thee, the Creator, to thee, the Powerful,
I offer this fresh bud,
New fruit of the ancient tree.
Thou art the master, we thy children.
Khmvoum [God], Khmvoum,
I offer this new plant.

Pygmy prayer

∼

HAIDA SONG

You came to me, you came to me.
You came walking to me, calling me "mother,"
instead of to someone else.
To me my child ... came walking,
calling me "mother."

The Haida people of the Northwest

GREETING TO THE NEWBORN

I am leading you to the crossroad.
See, this is your road to the market!
    This is your road when going for firewood!
    This is your road to the water place!
    This is your road to your farm!
    This is your road to your hometown!
May you grow up!
    And walk on it to the market,
    And walk on it for firewood,
    And walk on it to the water place,
    And walk on it to the farm,
    And walk on it to your hometown!
May the child stand fast on the ground!
May it grow strong!

The Krobo people of Ghana

NEWBORN SONG

To be sung by the one who first takes the child
from its mother

Newborn, on the naked sand
Nakedly lay it.
Next to the earth mother,
That it may know her,
Having good thoughts of her, the food giver.

Newborn, we tenderly
In our arms take it,
Making good thoughts.
House-god, be entreated,
That it may grow from childhood to manhood,
Happy, contented,
Beautifully walking
The trail to old age.
Having good thoughts of the earth its mother,
That she may give it the fruits of her being.
Newborn, on the naked sand
Nakedly lay it.

Pueblo song

In Indian home life ... there is no other tie to be compared in depth to that which binds together the mother and her child. With the coming of her first-born, be it boy or girl, the young wife has been advanced, as it were, out of the novitiate. She has become a member of the authoritative circle. It is as if the whole world recognizes that henceforth there will be one soul at least to whom her every act is holy.

Sister Nivedita, The Web of Indian Life

∽

Our God and God of our fathers, preserve this child to his father and to his mother.... Let the father rejoice in his offspring, and the mother be glad with the fruit of her body.

Jewish prayer

∽

I think my life began with waking up and loving my mother's face.

George Eliot, Daniel Deronda

INTO THE VOCATION OF MOTHERHOOD YOU HAVE CALLED ME

Words on Postpartum Depression

Into the vocation of motherhood you have called me.
Yet sorrow seems to be my only companion.
Sleeplessness.
Despondency.
A bitterness and grief.
This privilege of parenthood is a haunting.

Into the vocation of motherhood you have called me.
But I want none of it.
None.
Fear.
Dread.
Alarm.
Give me a long sleep and then maybe I'll think
    about it next year.
This I never signed up for.

Into the vocation of motherhood you have called me.
But I know your mistake.
I am not meant for such as this.
Am I?
Could I?
Might I?
How?
Give me the longest sleep and maybe,
maybe,
perhaps,
possibly,
I'll lift up my head, open my eyes,
And there she'll be.

Rev. Lauren J. McFeaters

No one tells you the really interesting stuff when you're pregnant. No one tells you, for instance, that your life is effectively over: that you're never going to draw another complacent breath again, and that the terror of losing your child arrives within 20 minutes of first seeing his or her face. No one mentions that whatever level of hypochondria and rage you'd learned to repress and live with is going to seem like the good old days about three weeks after your baby's arrival. There are good things they don't tell you, too, like how vibrational new babies are, how healing they are when they sleep on your chest, how you let out your breath and rest down into them and are set free of everything bad for just a moment. No one prepares you for how much joyousness babies elicit in you, in awful finicky old you, what unexpected capacities for twinkliness and softness and courage. But then again, no one tells you that sometimes you won't even like your child. Or that you are going to discover streaks of self-obsession and neuroses that make your crabby Aunt Nancy look like Meher Baba. No one, while discussing parenthood, ever mentions the word "pathological." Or "The Zone," a place of held-breath twilight terror when you can't locate your child.

So when our children got bigger and we looked back at our expectations—the Gerber commercial moments, the slow-motion footage on beaches and carousels, the TV sitcom moments of adorable mischief and softhearted exasperation—it's no wonder we decompensated into hysterical laughter. It's no wonder the tears streamed down our faces.

Anne Lamott, "Sleeping In"

~

Before you were conceived
    I wanted you
Before you were born
    I loved you
Before you were here an hour
    I would die for you
This is the miracle of life.

Maureen Hawkins, "The Miracle"

HEART'S CHILD

In Honor of My Adopted Daughter

Pink roses I'd fashioned from air
would be no less mysterious
than the new gold and pink daughter,
where once there was none,
who smiles, sleeping, in my arms.

In a wondrous greening of my soul,
I am no longer just me, I am a mother.
Ah, but more than a mere splitting of cells
in the tapestry of a womb, my daughter
and I are chambers in one another's hearts.

Margaret Anne Huffman

～

Whether severely wounded or just slightly so, mothers
have the potential to be the first sacrament — a tangible,
visible sign of God's intangible, invisible love — in the
lives of their children.

Kathleen Finley, The Liturgy of Motherhood

We welcome [Asher] into our lives and receive him as our beloved. He is a precious gift and we give thanks. You brought him into our family and made him part of us. We ache for him and delight in him. We celebrate every hair on his head and every breath that he takes.

We thank you for his birth mother, who brought him into this world, and pray for her family. May they experience your love and your beauty.

Heal any hurts from the past. Help him walk in the confusion, pain, and joy of his life before he came to us, knowing that you were with him in all of that. May he know that you are with him now and forever. Give us the humility, love, patience, and community to be good parents. Amen.

Janeen Steer

~

Mother's love is ever in its spring.

Anonymous

We have been blessed with the precious gift of this child. After so much waiting and wishing, we are filled with wonder and with gratitude as we call you our son/daughter. Our son/daughter, our child, you have grown to life apart from us, but now we hold you close to our hearts and cradle you in our arms with love. We welcome you into the circle of our family and embrace you with the beauty of a rich tradition.

We pledge ourselves to the creation of a Jewish/loving home and to a life of compassion for others, hoping that you will grow to cherish and emulate these ideals.

God of new beginnings, teach us to be mother and father, worthy of this sacred trust of life. May our son/daughter grow in health, strong in mind and kind in heart, a lover of Torah/learning, a seeker of peace. Bless all of us together within Your shelter of Shalom.

Rabbi Sandy Eisenberg Sasso

~

Maternal love is our first taste of love, the origin of all feelings of love. Our mother is the teacher who first teaches us love, the most important subject in life.

Thich Nhat Hanh, A Rose for Your Pocket

THANKSGIVING PRAYER FOR THE BIRTH PARENTS

God, who is both mother and father to us,
thank you for the gift that we have been given
through the selflessness of our child's birth
        parents.
It can't have been an easy decision for them to
        give her up,
and that decision has changed the lives of many
        people.

Please be with them and give them comfort,
both now and when they need it in the future—
at the times when they think about this child
and wonder how she is.

Help them to know that we will care for her well
and will help her to always be grateful to them
for the gift of her life.
Please bless her parents richly
and give them all that they need;
they have shared a most precious gift with us.
Amen.

Kathleen Finley

THE GIFT

A special little girl was born early in the morn
in another time and place.
Wanting the very best for her,
knowing I couldn't give enough,
it was the hardest decision I ever made.
In my heart I knew it was my only gift
to one so small,
hoping beyond hope she would understand,
hoping she might forgive.

Christine Ryan Paulus

~

Why so impatient my heart?
He who watches over birds, beasts, and insects,
He who cared for you
    whilst you were yet in your mother's womb,
Shall He not care for you
    now that you are come forth?

Kabir, fifteenth-century mystic poet of India

THE BEGINNING

"Where have I come from, where did you pick me up?" the baby asked its mother.

She answered half crying, half laughing, and clasping the baby to her breast, — "You were hidden in my heart as its desire, my darling.

You were in the dolls of my childhood's games; and when with clay I made the image of my god every morning, I made and unmade you then.

You were enshrined with our household deity, in his worship I worshipped you.

In all my hopes and my loves, in my life, in the life of my mother you have lived.

In the lap of the deathless Spirit who rules our home you have been nursed for ages.

...

As I gaze on your face, mystery overwhelms me; you who belong to all have become mine."

Rabindranath Tagore, The Crescent Moon

A PRAYER FOR NURSING

God, our mother,
you who nurture and cherish us,
nourish my child with my milk (this food).
Strengthen our love for one another,
from this day forth and forevermore.
Amen.

Rev. Lauren J. McFeaters

~

While nursing her child:

"I'm holding you, and God's holding me. I'm feeding
you, and God's feeding me." It was at these moments of
prayer that I began to perceive God as the source of all
motherly love, giving me the warmth, safety, and nourishment I needed to hand on to my child.

Margaret Hebblethwaite, Motherhood and God

COLOSTRUM

For four days, the baby's parched lips
worked my stinging skin. Pressed up beside me,
he suckled away our sleep
with his thirst. Those hospital nights
filled with the shrugs of nurses,
and ragged dreams of barren riverbeds,
    receding tides
and always the child in my arms,
shrinking slowly, a small sack of wailing.

The end of the fourth day,
my breasts suddenly transformed
into throbbing stones, yet still no milk.
In the shower, heat pelted away at the ache
while I willed hardness to melt.
Then they came, those rich yellow drops
my body had made and could finally offer,
the first sprinkle of rain on hungry soil,
and I watched my child with the eyes of all mothers
through fierce histories of loving and fear—
war-time queues, futile miles to a muddy well,
dirt sifted and sifted again
to find the stray kernels of corn
to pound into flour for the family's
single precious meal of the day.

Fiona Tinwei Lam

UPON HER SOOTHING BREAST

Upon her soothing breast
She lulled her little child;
A winter sunset in the west,
A dreary glory smiled.

Emily Brontë

~

Ask of her, the mighty mother:
Her reply puts this other
Question: What is Spring? —
Growth in everything.

Gerard Manley Hopkins,
"The May Magnificat"

3

Summer

A Season of Growth and Transformation

Summer is the season of transformation and abundant growth—a fitting metaphor for the evolving nature of the mother-child relationship. Gardeners spend the early days of summer thinning seedlings and letting others grow untouched. But in the heat of summer, the living takes over. The daisies that my sons planted from small clay pots leap the boundaries of our garden like a white wild fire.

Within this "Summer" section, writers explore how the mother-child relationship changes through daily interactions, separation, aging, encounters of brokenness, and healing. From varied faith traditions and backgrounds, these words express universal sentiments and illumine the many paradoxes of motherhood.

In the Buddhist tradition there is a teaching that "Samsara and Nirvana are not two, but one"—that suffering and paradise are inseparable. This is so true of motherhood. From the moment my sons were born, I loved them with my life. I nursed them and comforted them through nights of illness. I sang to them and witnessed their first smiles. Yet through it all, they were slowly moving away from me. The early, intimate attachment between mothers and children is bound by love, yet it is this very same devotion that eventually helps children separate from their mothers. And somehow this makes my affection for my sons all the more sacred and intense. In the words of Mother Teresa, "True love hurts, it always has to hurt."

In India, Hindu mothers participate in the ritual *phala dana trata*, "giving of her fruit to the world." This ritual takes place over several years and marks the transition of a mother releasing her child to the world. American culture does not offer such a formal ritual, but it is important to recognize that many mothers experience this transition as a loss, and, as with any loss, it is natural to grieve. This experience, which is both sad and freeing, transforms a mother's role. As Julian of Norwich states, the mother "changes her methods, not her love."

In a Mother's Day letter written from my father to my mother nearly forty years ago, he wrote of witnessing "a breast ignored for a smile." Reading of my own weaning sheds light on this life passage of which I have no conscious memory: one pleasure exchanged for another, one step away from the close embrace but one new way of connecting. And as my own mother witnessed in the smile of her infant, there will be small consolations in the letting go. One of the greatest challenges of motherhood is releasing expectations and allowing our children the space to grow into the people they naturally are.

Recently, a friend shared her anguish over her teenage daughter's erratic behavior. Within a matter of weeks, her daughter had her hair cut very short, dyed it purple, and turned against her faith. This mother ultimately realized that the most important thing she could do for her daughter was to "stay close to her," be present and available, even when such intimacy brought pain. This is good advice for any season of motherhood. Many of the writers in this "Summer" section offer words of hope that, in spite of the challenges we experience and mistakes we make as mothers, there will be moments of sacred connection.

Whether parenting a newborn or a young adult, motherhood is at once draining and a source of renewal. Women feel depleted, even devoured, but also fed and nourished by the intimate relationship with their children. Rising in the middle of the night to care for my feverish son exhausts me to the point of delirium, but in those moments of connection, I feel replenished with the love I'll need to return at his next cry.

The intimate relationships we develop with our children will be tried by the summer season of rain, drought, and unexpected storms. But, as the writers in this section express, the season also promises the brightest sun.

A MOTHER'S SONG

It is so still in the house,
There is a calm in the house;
The snowstorm wails out there,
And the dogs are rolled up with snouts under
    the tail.
My little boy is sleeping on the ledge,
On his back he lies, breathing through his
    open mouth.
His little stomach is bulging round—
Is it strange if I start to cry with joy?

Anonymous Eskimo woman

~

Paradise is at the foot of the mother.

The Prophet Muhammad

~

The mother-child relationship is paradoxical and, in a sense, tragic. It requires the most intense love on the mother's side, yet this very love must help the child grow away from the mother, and to become fully independent.

Erich Fromm, The Sane Society

If one but realized it, with the
onset of the first pangs of birth pains,
one begins to say farewell to one's baby.
For no sooner has it entered the world,
when others begin to demand their
share. With the child at one's breast,
one keeps the warmth of possession a
little longer.

Princess Grace of Monaco

~

Knowing that our God *is* there for our children, in
ways that we can never be, can help us when it comes
to the challenge of gradually letting go of our children,
but it still doesn't make that process easy. Letting go is
something we can't escape as mothers, no matter how
hard we try; our children start leaving us from the
moment they're born.

Kathleen Finley, The Liturgy of Motherhood

~

The mother must know when to let go the hand.

Chinese proverb

SEIZURE

For Howard Rabinowitz, Jack's doctor

I gave you what I could when you were born,
salt water to rock you,
your half of nine month's meat,
miles of finished veins,
and all the blood I had to spare.

And then I said, this is the last time
I divide myself in half, the last time
I lie down in danger and rise bereft,
the last time I give up half my blood.

Fifteen months later, when I walked into
    your room
your mobile of the sun, moon,
and stars was tilting
while your lips twisted,
while you arched your back.

Your fingers groped for something in the air.
Your arms and legs flailed like broken wings.
Your breath was a load too heavy
for your throat to heave into your lungs.
You beat yourself into a daze against your crib.

We slapped your feet,
we flared the lights,
we doused you in a tub of lukewarm water.
But your black eyes rolled.
You had gone somewhere
and left behind a shape of bluish skin,
a counterfeit of you.

It was then,
before the red wail of the police car,
before the IVs, before the medicine
dripped into you like angels, before you woke
to a clear brow, to your own funny rising voice,

it was then I would have struck the bargain,
all my blood for your small shaking.
I would have called us even.

Jeanne Murray Walker

WISDOM

Now I know why I've received the light of twenty summers on me, and why I've been given to picking flowers along the fields. Why, I asked myself on the most beautiful days, this marvelous gift of the warm sun and fresh grass?

As if I were a cluster of blue grapes, the light passed slowly through me, to deliver its sweetness. This which is making itself deep within me, drop by drop from my own veins, this was my wine.

For this one I prayed, so the name of God would pass through my clay, from which he would be made. And when I read a verse with trembling hands, He made my beauty burn like a red hot coal, so He could gather, for this child, his inextinguishable ardor from my flesh.

Gabriela Mistral

The mother's affection, by its very nature, grows deeper with deep need, and follows the beloved even into hell. A yearning love that can never refuse us; a benediction that forever abides with us; a presence from which we cannot grow away; a heart in which we are always safe; sweetness unfathomed, bond unbreakable, holiness without a shadow—all these indeed, and more, is motherhood.

Sister Nivedita, The Web of Indian Life

~

THE GIFT

my child ...

Young is your life, your path long, and you drink the love we bring you at one draught and turn and run away from us ...

We, indeed, have leisure enough in old age to count the days that are past, to cherish in our hearts what our hands have lost for ever.

The river runs swift with a song, breaking through all barriers. But the mountain stays and remembers, and follows her with his love.

Rabindranath Tagore, The Crescent Moon

THERE ARE TIMES IN LIFE
WHEN ONE DOES THE RIGHT THING

the thing one will not regret,
when the child wakes crying "Mama," late
as you are about to close your book and sleep
and she will not be comforted back to her crib,
she points you out of her room, into yours,
you tell her, "I was just reading here in bed,"
she says, "Read a book,"

    you explain it's not a children's book
but you sit with her anyway,

    she lays her head on your breast,
one-handed, you hold your small book,

    silently read,
resting it on the bed to turn pages
and she, thumb in mouth, closes her eyes, drifts,
not asleep—

    when you look down at her, her lids open,
and once you try to carry her back
but she cries,

    so you return to your bed again and book,
and the way a warmer air

    will replace a cooler with a slight
shift of wind, or swimming,

entering a mild current, you
enter this pleasure, the quiet book,
    your daughter in your lap,
an articulate person now, able to converse, yet still
her cry is for you, her comfort in you,
it is your breast she lays her head upon,
you are lovers,
    asking nothing but this bodily presence.
She hovers between sleep, you read your book,
you give yourself this hour,
    sweet and quiet beyond flowers
beyond lilies of the valley and lilacs even,
    the smell of her breath,
the warm damp between her head and your breast.
    Past midnight
she blinks her eyes,
    wiggles toward a familiar position,
utters one word, "sleeping."
    You carry her swiftly into her crib,
cover her, close the door halfway,
    and it is this sense of rightness,
that something has been healed, something
you will never know, will never have to know.

Ellen Bass

WHAT YOU HAVE CAUGHT AND HELD

For Eli

After I have carried you to your bed
for the third time and again I hear you
at my study door, I pretend not to notice.
Busy myself with the poem I am trying to end.

Thinking if I don't actually see you
maybe you won't really be there, in your blue
Superman pajamas and bare feet.
My body wilts over my desk

bruised from lack of sleep and the constant
touch of small boys kneading me. Bruised
on the inside like a plum held high and dropped.
You move along my shelves of books,

hands cupped, until you find what you are after.
Opening your father's cedar box,
you place what you hold, inside.
The lid falls with a wooden click.

"A dragonfly for my box," you whisper
shuffling out. Pretending my chair stands empty.
There's nothing there, I tell myself. No silver
wings. No trapped insect picking at the brass lock.

But when the pulse of the house slows
and I know you have wandered off to sleep
with your fat cat and net of dreams,
I crack the lid, find what I knew I would.

Bags of black cherry tobacco,
a book of spent matches, your
father's worn pipe. But who's to say
there isn't something more?

I drop the lid.
Afraid I'll be the one to let
what you have caught and held
escape.

Lynn L. Caruso

Creator God,
Give me the patience and wisdom to truly know
    my son.
To be present for him through all of life's joys
and trials. To understand his desires and needs.
To love him fully, yet allow him to live his own life.
And when I grow weary,
I surrender this work of parenting to you.
Renew my spirit so that I might begin
each day as the first. Amen.

Lynn L. Caruso

~

WORDS WRITTEN ON BEHALF OF YOUR THREE SMALL CHILDREN

Without you there would be no life
You have brought us into existence
And you have fed us with your own existence
You are that meal without which
    we would all starve.

Dr. Donald H. Liebert

Editor's Note: This excerpt is from a Mother's Day letter found in my mother's hope chest. The lines were written by my father nearly forty years ago.

It was a crisp cool morning at the city.
My mom and I saw the bakers busy at work.
As we entered the bakery
we heard the birds singing
        through the thin windows,
and the coins jingling in my pocket,
like jingle bells at Christmas.
My mom held my hand
and we walked to the case full of treats.
As I put the coins on the counter, she handed me
a steaming cinnamon roll with a fork. I took a bite.
In the bite I could have tasted my mom's heart.
In that sweet bite I also tasted
        the warm brown sugar.
I felt the soft dough on my tongue,
and smelled the warm cinnamon.
As if Love walked in the bakery
and said *What do you know?*
and I said,
This mom.

Sophia Waldenberg, age 8

PRAYER OF A SINGLE PARENT

My Lord and Holy Companion,
    I am alone in the awesome task
      of making a home.
I ask Your holy help
    to show me how
      to take on the responsibilities
    of both mother and father.
Direct my heart
    so that I may dispense the qualities
      of both parents,
    of gentle compassion on one hand,
    of firm discipline on the other;
    may I transmit true tenderness
      coupled with true strength.
These twin talents of the masculine and feminine
    are both within me,
    but it is difficult, Lord,
    to balance their daily expression in our home.
The days are long and the nights lonely,
    yet, with Your divine support,
    the impossible will unfold as possible,
    and our home will be more than a house.

My efforts to be two persons
    find my time directed to a great degree
    toward the needs of others;
    yet I, as well, am in need of comfort and love.
Let my prayer,
    my Lord and Secret One,
    renew my energy
    and remind me that I am not alone.
For you, my Lord, are with me!
The pathway of tomorrow is hidden from me;
    perhaps it is just as well.
May the unknown future
    only cast me into deeper trust and love of You
    and fill my heart
    with love enough for two. Amen.

Fr. Edward Hays

PRAYER FOR THOSE WHO CHOOSE ADOPTION

God of the Universe:

We pray for birth mothers. We ask for informed maturity, compassionate ears and shoulders, and tough love to help them make good choices for themselves and their children. Comfort those who grieve and give them faith and confidence in the future.

We pray for foster mothers. We give thanks for the willing hands and hearts of those who choose to care for babies and children in foster care. Give them patience and understanding and wisdom for the role they have chosen as temporary and long-term caretakers of little people.

We pray for the families who find joy and fulfillment in choosing to adopt. Be with those who come to terms with the pain of infertility, and inspire all of us who have room in our hearts and homes to include children with special needs in our families.

Bless all our children and families, and grant that we may find and reflect your love as we care for each other.

Amen.

Jackie Heil, foster mother to more than one hundred babies

BLESSING FOR A STEPPARENT

Tender God,
bless this parent whose bond with this child
is one of love, not of blood.
Give this parent all the wisdom that is needed
to be a faithful presence of love in this child's life —
not taking the place of the biological parent,
but being an extra source and reflection
of your love for this child.

Please give this parent special graces
for the difficult challenges that may lie ahead;
give abundantly of your care, patience, and
    acceptance
so that she or he may be a source
of those qualities in this child's life
and to help this child to know
that there are no limits and exclusions to real love.
Amen.

Kathleen Finley

DEAR GOD, BLESS ALL MOTHERS ...
especially those whose children are starting school today

Up until the first day of school, God, the mothers of these tiny people have been their main resource for direction, authority, information, security, and tender-loving care. But, starting today, God, everything will be different. Today these "babies" begin to shed their parental dependency and embrace new teachers, make new friends, and do things that their mothers don't even know they are doing. Today is the first of many letting-go-days in the life of every mother, God. Grant her peace by realizing that you are in school with her child, even though she is not. Thank you, God, for your care of school children everywhere. Amen.

Lauren McLaughlin

~

A kind, loving mother, who understands and knows the needs of her child will look after it tenderly because it is the nature of a mother to do so. As the child grows older, she changes her methods, not her love. This way of doings things is our Lord at work in those who do them. Thus God is our Mother.

Julian of Norwich, Revelations of Divine Love

MOTHERLOVES

Off-center and still shaken from the throw
onto the slowly spinning Potter's wheel,
the clay had scarcely time to wonder, so
quickly did the hands begin to feel
the shape and heal the cracks and now to shift
the hopeless lumpy mass back from the side
and, yes, into the center, and to lift
it toward a shape it had no need to hide.
To see the ragged edges smoothed at last,
to see a form emerge, new shape begun,
was finally to see the painful past
transformed into a new life for my son.
I cannot guide the hand, or see the face
of love the Potter has, but know her grace.

Bishop Margaret G. Payne

PARK

The mother closes her eyes a half minute
so her eyelids can fall
even if the rest of her can't.

She leans against the stroller,
an incarnation of torpor
pushing a strapped-in toddler
across blasts of car exhaust
up a marathon incline.

They arrive finally
at the bounded universe of sand and grass,
the timeless calls and cries
of children spinning and clambering
within discrete pockets of glee,
thuds and skids of their balls and boards,
parental pleas and cautionings
blending and muting in the air
of summer's end.

She places him in the sandbox.
Crouched on the sidelines
under a flicker of shade,
she pretends to monitor
the progress of his front end loader.

But he just wants to run
to the expanse of greenness, through to everything
that is openness.
He reaches up at a helicopter,
a small unity of bone, muscle and breath
aching for flight.

She gathers what is left of herself
to stand with him
to mark movement through the sky,
rising the way a mother must rise,
her weary loving face
on the perimeter of joy.

Fiona Tinwei Lam

~

A mother's love is like the tree of life
Strong in spirit
peaceful, wise and beautiful

African proverb

When Sam was a colicky baby, it was one thing. I felt free to discuss my terrible Caliban feelings because I was so exhausted and hormonal and without a clue as to how to be a real mother that I believed anyone would understand my feelings. I felt confused, though, that no one tells you when you're pregnant how insane you're going to feel after the baby comes, how pathological, how inept and out of control. Or how, when they get older, you'll still sometimes feel exhausted, hormonal, without a clue. You'll still find your child infuriating. Also—I am just going to go ahead and blurt this out— dull....

This is a closely guarded secret, as if the myth of maternal bliss is so sacrosanct that we can't even admit these feelings to ourselves. But when you mention these feelings to other mothers, they all say, "Yes, yes!" You ask, "Are you ever mean to your children?" "Yes!" "Do you ever yell so that it scares you?" "Yes, yes!" "Do you ever want to throw yourself down the back stairs because you're so bored with your child that you can hardly see straight?" "Yes, Lord, yes, thank you, thank you ... "

Anne Lamott, "Mother Rage: Theory and Practice"

The love of a mother for a child is the truest love around. Loving a child teaches us what real love is: selfless, patient and forgiving. We learn that love is unconditional, non-judgmental and expects little if anything in return. Of course there are times when we resent our children, when they put us in touch with the dark sides of our natures, but overall our relationship with them is one of overwhelming love. As one mother puts it:

After I had a child I realized that all the love I had experienced in the past—especially with partners—was selfish. I was constantly thinking, what's in this relationship for me? And if my expectations weren't met any good feeling would dry up altogether. My daughter has taken me to hell and back but there's nothing she can do to make me stop loving her.

Sarah Napthali, Buddhism for Mothers

~

I forgive my Children for any disrespect, temper tantrums, manipulation, hurts, especially _____. I release them from my judgments [and] make peace with them today. Bless them, Lord.

Fr. Robert DeGrandis,
The Ten Commandments of Prayer

DEAR GOD, BLESS ALL MOTHERS ...
especially mothers of teenagers

God, did you mean for the personalities of our children to change completely overnight? Somewhere, around the age of 13, mothers of teens find themselves living with little strangers. What does a mother do, God, when suddenly she can't do anything right? Show each mother of a teenager how to accept that her child has a natural desire to be independent. Remind her not to be threatened by that, because she once felt exactly the same way. Help her to find her own ground, so that she can strike a healthy balance between flexibility and steadfastness. Guide her to make sensible choices about her child's welfare, but never to engage in censorship. Thank you, God, for the unique ability you give to all mothers, to love their teenagers in spite of themselves. Amen.

Lauren McLaughlin

~

Give, I pray thee, to all children grace reverently to love their parents, and lovingly obey them. Teach us all that filial duty never ends or lessens; and bless all parents in their children, and all children in their parents.

Christina Rossetti

A mother best serves her child who serves herself.

The Buddha

~

ETERNAL PAIN

I grow pale if he suffers inside me. I'm becoming full of pain from his hidden pressure, and I could die from a single movement of this one I don't see.

But don't think he'll only be woven with my soul while I keep watch over him. When he wanders freely out in the streets, even though far away, the wind that lashes at him will tear my flesh and his cry will also rise in my throat. My tears and my smile will begin in your face, my child!

Gabriela Mistral

~

A mother understands what a child does not say.

Jewish proverb

A BOWL OF SOUP,
Bergen-Belsen Concentration Camp, April 1945

Shortly before the liberation of Bergen-Belsen on April 15, 1945, both Rosalie and Jolly expected to die. Neither shared her premonition with the other. Jolly volunteered for work to earn a precious extra food ration. For a day of digging pits to bury some of the thousands of inmates who had died of malnutrition or disease, she "earned" a bowl of soup, which she brought back for her mother.

[In a video testimony] Jolly Z related:

And somehow I found the barrack where she was waiting for me. [Putting her arm around Rosalie] And when I came in, I said, "Look, mother, I have a bowl of soup." And she said, "I don't want any. You eat it." I said, "I had already a bowl." She says, "No, I want you to survive. You are young. I had my life already." And I said, "Please, no, you have to survive. Father will be waiting, my brother will be waiting. We both have to survive." So we decided to share it. My mother took a spoon, but the spoon was empty. She hardly took anything. And when I took a spoon, it was also empty, because I didn't want to take much that she should have.

So we realized that we're not getting anywhere, and we decided to feed each other. So she was feeding me, and I was feeding her. And that bowl of soup most likely really saved us, because in a day or two we were liberated.

Johanna Bodenstab, "Under Siege: A Mother-Daughter Relationship Survives the Holocaust"

~

To raise an infant, to look after it, to educate it, and to give oneself to its service is as much and as good as the work of an adept because an adept forgets himself in meditation and a mother forgets herself by giving her life to the child.

Sufi master Hazrat Inayat Khan,
The Art of Personality

FOR THE LOVE OF A CHILD

parenthood is a challenge
a trial by fire
enduring little words
of hate of love
changing with the winds
hot dry simoons that leave you
sweltering a monsoon of tears
or staked out thirsty
for a gentle touch
a bit of respite

motherhood is a gauntlet
tidals and eddies
rocked to the core when a child
throws up your nurturing
words of wisdom
blood you have bled
nailing you as you nailed
your mother before
your own hand at creation

grit across deserts
of things not said
hotly said mostly said
settle in eyes
washed to the soul
for the love of a child

Trish Shields

~

AT THE END OF SPRING

The flower of the pear-tree gathers
    and turns to fruit;
The swallows' eggs have hatched
    into young birds.
When the Seasons' changes
    thus confront the mind
What comfort can the Doctrine of Tao give?
It will teach me to watch the days and months fly
Without grieving that Youth slips away.

Po Chü-i, Tang dynasty poet

Father-Mother, into your hands I commend my
    daughter,
As she goes off to college,
As our family changes beyond recognition.
This mothering thing is hard work,
And I'm just now beginning to get it right,
    Some of the time.
But you, Great God, created her well, and
    You got it right.
Yes, into your hands I commend my daughter,
My hopes, my fears, my smiles, my tears.
Keep loving her, Loving God, even more than I do.

Jane Richardson Jensen

~

ZUNI PRAYER

Now this is the day.
Our child,
Into the daylight
You will go out standing.
Preparing for your day,
We have passed our days.

Author unknown

FOR MY DAUGHTER ON HER TWENTY-FIRST BIRTHDAY

When they laid you in the crook
of my arms like a bouquet and I looked
into your eyes, dark bits of evening sky,
I thought, of course this is you,
like a person who has never seen the sea
can recognize it instantly.

They pulled you from me like a cork
and all the love flowed out. I adored you
with the squandering passion of spring
that shoots green from every pore.

You dug me out like a well. You lit
the deadwood of my heart. You pinned me
to the earth with the points of stars.

I was sure that kind of love would be
enough. I thought I was your mother.
How could I have known that over and over
you would crack the sky like lightning,
illuminating all my fears, my weaknesses, my sins.
Massive the burden this flesh
must learn to bear, like mules of love.

Ellen Bass

To my beautiful grown sons

ADAGIO

You appeared on my horizon,
a
tiny
glowing
Orb.

You expanded quickly
into a rainbow of colour,

impacting
my
Soul
and my Heart.

Each moment you shine more brightly,
Blinding
Searing.

The blindness from brightness viewed is Bliss.
The Soul's singing far sweeter from Ecstasy held.

The pain of longing comes full circle,
Just as the Sun ...
and the Moon ...
and the Stars.

Gloria Waggoner

When children left home in the Outer Isles of Scotland, their mothers whispered the following lines. These words were often remembered as the last accents of a mother's voice.

THE MOTHER'S BLESSING

Be the great God between thy two shoulders
To protect thee in thy going and in thy coming,
Be the Son of Mary Virgin near thine heart,
And be the perfect Spirit upon thee pouring—
Oh, the perfect Spirit upon thee pouring!

Gaelic mothers' consecration

~

My son
and his son
wade into their shadows

Winona L. Baker

FOR MY DAUGHTER'S
TWENTY-FIRST BIRTHDAY

I stroked her cheek with my finger
and she began to suck for dear life
like a fish in the last stages of suffocation
    above water.
When I poured my voice down to revive her
she grinned and graduated from college
Summa Cum Laude, schools of minnows
    parting before her.
"You are not a fish," I said to her.
"You are my daughter, and just born, too.
You should know your place.
At least we are going to start off right."
Like a woman whose hand
    has just been severed at the wrist
but who can still feel pain
    winking in the lost fingers,
I felt my stomach turn when she moved
    in her crib of seaweeds.
"Last month at this time," I said,
"you and my heart swam together
    like a pair of mackerel."
But she waved goodbye from a moving car,
hanging onto her straw hat with one hand,
light reflecting from the car window
as from an opened geode.

I wonder if she knows how I have stood for years
staring down through the fathoms between us
where her new body swims, paying out silver
    light.
It is as though I am still trying
to haul her up to me for food, for oxygen,
my finger in her mouth lodged like a hook.

Jeanne Murray Walker

~

ON A CHILD'S STARTING SCHOOL

Teach me to let go, Lord:
to let my child take his own steps into the big
    world,
to watch and care but to let him grow,
as you, Lord, let us all grow, all of us your children.
You let us make our own choices, our own
    mistakes,
although you love us — because you love us.
He is ours, Lord, yours and mine; upheld by both
    our loves.
We both want the best for him.
Let him be sure of that, now and wherever he goes.

Rev. Dr. Henry McKeating

For my mother and her grandson Samuel

I move through her house calling their names,
thinking they have walked to the river,
the August sun heavy over the valley.

The house is still. Even the ticking of the carved
clock slows in the heat. Then I find them,
my son asleep with his grandmother.

Her bed, a small pond.
Their bodies, two warm stones
in a ring of tossed sheets.

As I watch, his arm moves over his sweaty
hair in a long, deep dive. His mouth open
as if calling out to her.

Her smooth hands reach to touch
the curve of his back, to check
that he still swims beside her.

Below the cool surface he dreams of stepping
off the rail of the river's bridge. She dreams
of catching. This woman, this small boy —

a summer fairy tale.
As if walking through the thick forest
into a clearing, and brushing aside the green

ferns and branches, I finally find
what I didn't know
I was even after.

Lynn L. Caruso

A NAP IN MY MOTHER'S HOUSE

From the guest bed I hear her.
The delicate tick
Of feet bones
As she steps
Around the house
Placing one thing
And another.

Laundry spins
And rolls
In distant machines.
Twin galaxies
Of remote
And clanking orbits.

I can sleep here.

Sometimes I hear
The sprinklers hiss,
Awaking
At their appointed times.

A time for each routine.
A place for each thing.
She delivers a warm stack of towels
To my door.

Lauri Hewitt

4

Autumn
A Season of Thanks-Giving

H istorically, autumn rituals and ceremonies connected humankind to the natural world and to the Divine. They were a time to both celebrate the harvest and offer thanks-giving to the sun god, or Mother Earth, who sustains us. Today, autumn continues to be the season when we recognize our interconnection with both the earth and our Creator, offering gratitude for the gifts received from both. Author Anita Diamant describes the unique connection that women have with the earth and the Divine, as she reflects on the ancient Jewish belief that "the ebb and flow of the cycles" within women's bodies make them "watchful, mindful of the gifts of heaven and earth."

Autumn rituals recognize the transformation from seed to flower to fruit, and this section offers ceremonies celebrating the parallel physical and spiritual experiences in motherhood.

Several years ago, a close friend spent months carrying a grainy photograph of the Guatemalan boy she longed to adopt. When he finally arrived, I wanted her baby shower to include a blessing as unique as their situation. This one-year-old Guatemalan boy joined this single woman and became, in that instant, family. I located a Mayan birth ritual from his native Guatemala that fit the occasion perfectly. Through the symbolic lighting of four candles, we welcomed this little boy into the four corners of our community, pledging our maternal support and honoring the light of God's presence.

Whether through adoption or birth, the arrival of a new child is a sacred occasion. Within this "Autumn" section there are four original, multifaith ceremonies—including the Guatemalan ritual—that offer thanksgiving for the blessings inherent in new motherhood. These ceremonies can be used as presented, incorporated into a formal rite of sacred initiation within your own faith tradition, or included in a baby shower to add a spiritual richness to the event. There is also an additional ceremony to mark the experience of weaning a child.

The ceremonies within "Autumn" honor not only the intimate relationship between parent and child but also the significance of community. I remember one overwhelming week of missing work and sleepless nights, tending to my sick two-year-old. After many exhausting days my good friend Deb knocked on my door and insisted that my son come to her house so I could finally have a break. It is on these most difficult of days that community sustains us.

Autumn is a time when gardeners reflect on the challenges and accomplishments of the past year and prepare for the next season. Traditionally in American culture, women gather for baby showers in much the same way—reflecting together on past shared experiences, while looking ahead to the new season.

When we gather in community to celebrate and greet a new life, we are also greeting one another. *Namaste* is a Hindi word that is translated as "I honor the Light of life in you." Through this one-word greeting, individuals honor the interconnection and sacredness of all, while at the same time recognizing the Divine source of that interconnection. This greeting resounds through all of the ceremonies offered in this section.

So, *welcome. Namaste.* May all who participate in these ceremonies gather in a spirit of gratitude and may

the blessing of God our Mother
give you strength for the journey,
light for the path,
and illumination for the way to come.

Rev. Lauren J. McFeaters

SONG OF THE CHILD
A Blessing Ceremony for the Expectant Mother and Child

INVITATION

In the beginning, all creatures were hidden treas-
ures—longing to be known, and brought into being.
God then exhaled a sigh of compassion, and with that
great sigh, the world was created.

Sufi parable

SACRED TEXT READINGS

Homage to you, Breath of Life, in our birth
and in our death. In the whole cycle of life you
sustain and inspire us.

The Atharva-Veda, c. 1500

~

The spirit of God has made me, and the breath
of the Almighty gives me life.

Job 33:4

I am the Mother of the Voice, speaking in many ways, completing the All. It is in me that knowledge dwells, the knowledge of things everlasting. It is I who speak within every creature.

> *Words spoken by the female Logos in*
> *Gnostic literature*

REFLECTION

In East Africa there is a tribe with a very unique ritual surrounding conception and birth. In preparation for conceiving a child, a woman leaves her community and sits alone beneath a tree, where she remains in prayer and meditation until she has received her child's "song." This song is later taught to her husband before conception and sung to her child throughout pregnancy.

Each child's song is unique and will be sung by the midwives who welcome each child at birth. But perhaps most powerfully, every child's song will be learned by members of the child's village and will accompany them throughout their lives. It will be sung to soothe them when injured and to celebrate many joyous rites of passage. It will resound at marriage ceremonies. And at the end of life, villagers will gather, as they did at birth, to sing them from this world.

Just as the East African woman is open to receiving words for her child's song, this ritual offers an opportunity for the expectant mother to begin to hear her own child's song. In this ceremony the mother will receive written blessings to take with her. She could later use these words as inspiration for her child's song, which may take the form of a poem, letter, story, prayer, or actual lyrics.

"SONG OF THE CHILD" BLESSING

While listening to a piece of instrumental music, invite participants to write down a blessing or wish for the unborn child. Let them know that they will be completing the Mother's Prayer, which ends with this line: "May his/her song be of ... " They can write whatever they hope will fill this child's life: good friends, family, adventures.

With participants seated in a circle, pass around a long ribbon, piece of leather, or string until each guest holds a section. This act symbolically links each person with the expectant mother and with one another.*

The expectant mother then reads the "Mother's Prayer." The mother may wish to insert her own blessing before others read what they have written. It is particularly meaningful to include a reference to ancestors who, even in their absence, will influence who this child will become. For example, the mother might say, "May her [his] song be of [insert names], strong ancestors who left their home in [insert country] to travel to a foreign land."

---

* *Idea adapted from* Welcoming the Soul of a Child *by Jill E. Hopkins*

MOTHER'S PRAYER

To be spoken by the expectant mother

Creator God,
In these final days of waiting for my child,
I turn to you for wisdom in motherhood.
You cradle her before she is even born,
sing to her in the rush of my blood,
and you will hold her when her days are done.

Teach me the words to my daughter's lullaby.
May her song always serve to remind her
of who she is and from where she's come.

Now I close with this blessing;
May her song be of [insert family names].

Lynn L. Caruso

PARTICIPANTS' BLESSINGS

When the mother has completed her prayer, other participants read their wish/blessing. As each one concludes, she cuts her length of string and ties it into a bracelet to wear until the baby's birth. Encourage each guest to hold the mother and child in her thoughts and prayers whenever she sees the bracelet. The circle of the bracelet is symbolic of the circle of community gathered for this occasion.

COMMUNITY PRAYER

Lord God,
You have given mothers to the world and
blessed the fruit of their womb ... Hear, O
Lord, our prayer and bless the mother of this
home. Grant her strength to fulfill her calling.
May she be filled with joy and laughter.
May she experience peace of mind and heart,
and may her children rise up to bless her ...
Amen.

Robert E. Webber, Mother's Day Blessing

CLOSING

Leader: I add my breath to your breath

**All: That our days may be long on the Earth....
That we may finish our roads together**

Leader: May our Mother bless you with life

All: May our Life Paths be fulfilled.

Song of the Pueblo people

❦

DAR A LUZ
A Blessing Ceremony for the Expectant Mother and Child

INVITATION

> May the blessing of light be on you,
> light without and light within.
> May the blessed sunshine shine on you
> and warm your heart
> till it glows like a great peat fire,
> so that the stranger may come
> and warm himself at it,
> and also a friend.
>
> *Irish blessing*

REFLECTION

In Spanish, the phrase *dar a luz* is used to describe childbirth. These words are literally translated as "to give to light." The metaphor of light representing the Divine is found in many faith traditions, and the following ceremony infuses this Spanish phrase with spiritual meaning.

PRAYER

To be spoken by expectant mother / parents. Insert "me"
and "I" if only expectant mother is present.

Creator God,
We come before you in thanksgiving.
You have trusted us to be partners with you
in this miracle of creation and we are grateful.
May we live each day ever mindful
of this covenant between us.
Just as the sun and the moon
have made their promises—
"I will watch the earth by day
I will guard her through the night"—
walk with us on this journey.
And in some small way,
may we reflect for our child
the light of your divine love.

In this child,
you have given us a gift unimaginable.
At this birth we return the giving;
we give [insert child's name]
to the light
dar a luz
Amen.

Lynn L. Caruso

SONG

Song for bringing a child into the world

You day-sun, circling around,
You daylight, circling around,
You night-sun, circling around.

Anonymous, Seminole, North American Indian

SACRED TEXT READINGS

[Allah] is the light of the heavens and the earth … glorified in the mornings and in the evenings (again and again).

Qur'an 35–36

~

God is light and in him there is no darkness at all.... If we walk in the light as he himself is in the light, we have fellowship with one another.

1 John 1:5, 7

NAMASTE BLESSING

Namaste is a Hindi word that is translated as "I now honor the Light of life within you." Through this one-word greeting, individuals honor the interconnection and sacredness of all.

For this blessing participants sit in a circle, each holding an unlit candle. Invite one person to light her candle from a central flame, which symbolizes the divine light, and offer a personal blessing, or wish, for the mother and child. This participant then lights the next person's candle, and she, too, offers a blessing. Continue until all are connected through this ritual lighting. As the light is passed, encourage participants to greet the person whose candle they are lighting by using the word *namaste*.

At the end of the ceremony, participants take their candles home, along with a list of guests' names. When the mother's labor begins, arrange for the first person on the list to be contacted, who in turn will contact the second on the list and so forth. Each of the participants will light her candle and hold the mother in prayer during her labor and delivery.

REFLECTION

The Blessingway is one of the central ceremonies of the Navajo people and is commonly held late in a woman's pregnancy. Traditionally, only women gather to participate in this sacred ceremony, which is intended to provide the mother with the strength she will need for labor. Giving birth is viewed as a deeply spiritual experience and is celebrated with a Blessingway to mark this significant rite of passage in a woman's life.

When a pregnant Navajo woman participates in the Blessingway, she is identifying with the original act of creation—expressing desire that her birth experience will imitate the "way" our Creator created and gave life. It is believed that the very act of participating in the ceremony endows the mother with these powers of creation.

CIRCLE OF BLESSING

The following adapted ceremony begins with these lines from an actual Navajo Blessingway, to be read at the start of the blessing.

With long life happiness surrounding me
    may I in blessing give birth!
    May I quickly give birth!

In blessing may I arise again,
    in blessing may I recover, as one
    who is long life happiness may I live on!

Before me may it be blessed,
    behind me ... below me ...
    above me ...
    in all my surroundings may it be blessed,
    may my speech be blessed!

It has become blessed again,
    it has become blessed again ...

Blessingway #15, Sacred Works

While still seated in a circle, ask participants to join in the following responsive blessing.

Mother: "With long life happiness surrounding me may I in blessing give birth! May I quickly give birth!"

All: In blessing may you give birth.

Mother: "In blessing may I arise again, in blessing may I recover."

All: In blessing may you recover.

Mother: "[In] long life happiness may I live on!"

All: In blessing may you live on.

Mother: "Before me may it be blessed, behind me, below me, above me, in all my surroundings may it be blessed."

All: Surrounded with the warmth of divine light, may you and your child be blessed.

Editor's note concerning cultural sensitivity: It is with great reverence and respect that I share the words of this Navajo Blessingway. Native American spirituality is a seamless part of their very lives and in removing the ceremony from its context, it is not possible to retain the power and sacredness of the ritual. The ceremony above is not presented as an actual Blessingway, but rather as an inspired adaptation.

PRAYER

> Creator God, you, who know this child
> > before he takes his first breath,
> hold him in your motherly love,
> > even as his mother
> > still holds him in her womb.
> May we trust in you.
> Trust in the knowledge
> > that what has been planted in shadow
> > will be sown into full sun.
> Bless this home, and family,
> > with the warmth of your holy light.
> Amen.
>
> *Lynn L. Caruso*

BENEDICTION

A BLESSING

> May the blessing of God our Mother
> give you strength for the journey,
> > light for the path,
> and illumination for the way to come.
>
> May the blessing of our heavenly Parent
> shower you with wisdom,
> > and intuition,
> > and a depth of understanding,
> from this day forth and forevermore.
>
> Go in God's peace.
>
> *Rev. Lauren J. McFeaters*

WELCOME FOR BIRTH
A Multigenerational Family Celebration

INVITATION

For a Newborn Child

I lift up this newborn child to you.
You brought it to birth, you gave it life.
This child is a fresh bud on an ancient tree,
A new member of an old family.
May this fresh bud blossom.
May this child grow up strong and righteous.

Kalahari Bushmen

GRANDPARENTS' PRAYER

If grandparents are not in attendance, invite other family members to read this prayer and adapt it accordingly.

Creator God,
We thank you for bringing this child into our family.
Today we offer our love and support
    to her parents,
    bless them in the days ahead.
And may we serve as caretakers
    of our granddaughter's history.

Keeping her ever mindful of our family's
    roots
that stretch into past generations
and fruit into future lives.
Amen.

Lynn L. Caruso

TRADITIONAL BLESSING

This traditional blessing is offered at the birth of a Muslim child.

You have been blessed in what you have been
given. May you give thanks to the One who
granted it. May your child reach maturity and
right-guidance, and may [Allah] make him a
blessing for you.

WELCOMING CEREMONY

The Jewish Brit E'dut ceremony welcomes the arrival
of a new daughter. In this ceremony the child is
wrapped in the *tallit* (prayer shawl) that her parents
were married under.

This ceremony could easily be adapted using a special
keepsake blanket or family quilt.

Parent:
As your father and I stood under the shelter of this *tallit*
to be joined together as husband and wife, so now do

we encircle you within it as you enter the circle of our family. As we wrap you in this *tallit*,* so may your life be wrapped in justice and righteousness. As we embrace you today, so may you embrace your tradition and your people.

Guest:
As your eyes are filled with wonder when you gaze at the world, so, too, may you be filled with wonder at the everyday miracles of life.

Guest:
As you startle to the world around you, so may you remain ever open both to the happiness and to the pain of those you encounter in the world.

Guest:
As you cry for food and comfort now, so may you one day cry out to correct the injustices of the world, to help clothe the naked and feed the hungry.

Guest:
As your hand tightly grasps your mother's finger, so may you grasp hold of learning and grow in knowledge and in wisdom.

Anita Diamant, The New Jewish Baby Book

---

* *If using a blanket or quilt, substitute the appropriate word for* tallit.

BLESSING OF THE PARENT(S) AND CHILD

The person reciting this blessing places one hand on the child and one on the parent(s). If grandparents are not present, simply omit paragraph three.

COVENANT CEREMONY

Reader:
You are your parents' dream realized, their hopes fulfilled. You are the latest and best chapter in the unfolding lives of your family.

Reader:
You are a bridge over which we who welcome you can gaze from this day into future days, from our generation into yours. You are the newest link in the endless chain of [our people's history].

Grandparents:
Our God and God of all generations, we are grateful for new beginnings, for the bond of new life that links one generation to another. Thankful for the blessings of family, for the love and care that bring meaning and happiness to our lives, we rejoice with our children at the birth of our grandchild.

All: Blessed are You, O God, who gives us life, who sustains us, and who brings us here to share in this occasion.

Reader: A new son of [Israel] has come, and with him comes a great promise. In his soul is the potential to bring greatness into our world. He brings blessing to our lives, as he reminds us that the world is not yet complete. We each share in the task of perfecting this world.

Anita Diamant, The New Jewish Baby Book

PRAYER

To be spoken by parent(s)

Creator God,
We pray that our son will live
his life
    with concern for the world around him.
With his birth we are reminded
    of the possibility for goodness
    in a world that is often filled with suffering.
Help us to be a part of the healing—
    renewing our commitment
    to repair the path ahead
    for his sake
    and for the sake of all God's children.
Amen.

Lynn L. Caruso

TIME OF THANKS-GIVING

Traditionally, in Jewish birth ceremonies a monetary gift called *tzedakah* (charity) is offered, often in the amount of the baby's weight. Parents could make such a donation to a children's charity and encourage guests to do the same.

TIME OF PLANTING

Guests could help plant a tree to mark the occasion of the child's birth. In ancient Jewish tradition, cedar was often selected for a son's birth and cypress or pine for a daughter's. It was customary for a couple's *chuppah* (wedding canopy) then to be made from the wood of their birth trees. The parents may want to select a tree that represents their child's birth month.

BENEDICTION

> The Lord bless you and keep you;
> the Lord make his face to shine upon you
> and be gracious to you,
> the Lord lift up his countenance upon you,
> and give you peace.
>
> *Numbers 6:24–26*

WELCOME FOR ADOPTION
A Blessing from Guatemala

SACRED TEXT READINGS

I have called you by name, you are mine.

Isaiah 43:1

~

I am — of all this boundless Universe —
The Father, Mother, Ancestor, and Guard!

Bhagavad Gita 9:17

PRAYER

To be spoken by parent(s)

Mother God,
Even before our first breath, you called us child.
Adopted into your family, nurtured by your love.
May we learn from your example.
We thank you for the amazing gift of our son.
For trusting us to be his parents —
     we are humbled.
You have brought this child into our family,
Completing the circle we had left open.

On this day, by this child, we are named.
Christened by him: *"Mother, Father."*
Help us learn what it means
    to carry these names.

And may he feel truly cherished.
Chosen, like you have chosen each of us,
Knowing he belongs, and has always belonged
In the circle of this family.
Amen.

Lynn L. Caruso

POEM

Pledge for an Adopted Child

> We did not plant you,
> True.
> But when the season is done,
> When the alternate prayers
> For the sun and for rain are counted,
> When the pain of weeding
> And the pride of watching are through,
> We will hold you high.
>
> A shining sheaf
> Above the thousand seeds grown wild
> Not by our planting,

But by heaven.
Our harvest.
Our own child.

Anonymous

REFLECTION

For the Mayans of Guatemala, a child's birth is celebrated by the entire community. It is believed that the child belongs not only to the parents, but also to all members of the village. When informed of a baby's arrival, individuals gather to pledge their support, promising to serve as second parents and calling themselves *abuelos* (grandparents) or ancestors of the child.

Four candles are placed around the bed to symbolize the four corners of the child's home and greater community, and it is believed that through their lighting, the child is drawn into the community and world in which the child will live.

WORDS OF BLESSING

Note: [M] and [C] indicate where the mother's and child's names should be inserted.

Light four candles and give each participant a small candle, a slip of paper, and a pen. Ask guests to write a blessing, thought, or wish for the mother and/or child and hold them until the end of the blessing. If the child is present, the mother cradles the infant in her arms as the blessing is offered.

Leader: [M] and [C], the friends and family who gather with you on this day represent the many "corners" of your world.

All: (Guests name their connection with the mother, such as friend, family, or co-worker.)

Leader: [C], we have awaited your arrival and rejoice that you are safely here.

All: We welcome you into our community. May you sense our presence in the days ahead.

Leader: [C], may you come to feel at home in our midst.

All: And in some small way, may we take on the roll of *abuelos* in your life.

Leader: [M], we light these candles to remind you of the warmth of the community gathered with you on this day.

[M] and [C], we offer our support as members of your community—as *abuelos*. Receive our blessing on this special day.

At this point, invite guests to share the blessings they have written. After reading their blessing, guests will tie their slip of paper to the candle with a piece of ribbon. At the end of the blessing, the mother takes these with her. Later, whenever she needs encouragement, the mother can read the blessings and light the candles. These blessings will serve to remind her of her community of support—the *abuelos* who walk beside her.

Prayer at Adoption

Gracious and loving God, like a mother you comfort us; like a father you care for us. You have looked upon us with compassion and goodness to have brought us to a time such as this....

We thank you for the gift of [C] and for leading us to her [him] and for leading [C] to us. You, who set us to live as families, are showing us the abundance of your love through this family. You, who have adopted us all as children, make manifest your grace through the true devotion and affection of this family.

Lord, as we assemble here, we thank you for this family; for their devotion that unites and does not divide and for their hope which strengthens and does not alienate. Give them a love that bears all things, believes all things, hopes all things and endures all things. Call them all to a strength and wisdom and insight as they begin the work of love and as they embark on the journey of a life together, a life with us, and a life with you.

We thank you for the love that these parents have for each other, and for the family they have raised in grace and in kindness. As hope is fulfilled among us tonight in the celebration of [C's] adoption, we thank you for the trust and nurture you have given each one here to set free their hearts and make room for one another. Amen.

Rev. Lauren J. McFeaters

PRAYER

To be spoken by the mother

Creator God,
Teach me, through your holy example
to be the mother whom you desire for this child.

Bless our home—
may it be a place of shelter.

Bless my arms—
may they embrace whoever she becomes.

Bless my body—
may it be a cradle to hold her throughout life.

Bless my voice—
may it fill her with stories of her place in our family.

Thank you for the women gathered here today.
Sustain me in this work of mothering,
ever mindful that on those days when I feel
depleted and overwhelmed, on days I fail,
there are other *abuelas* [grandmothers] who walk
    beside me.
Amen.

Lynn L. Caruso

BENEDICTION

Clasp him to your heart and bless him.
He has come into this land of a hundred cross-roads.
I know not how he chose you from the crowd,
    came to your door,
and grasped your hand to ask his way …
Keep his trust, lead him straight and bless him.
Lay your hand on his head, and pray
that though the waves underneath
    grow threatening,
yet the breath from above may come and
    fill his sails
and waft him to the haven of peace.
Forget him not in your hurry,
let him come to your heart and bless him.

Rabindranath Tagore, *The Crescent Moon*

A MEDITATION ON WEANING

SACRED TEXT READINGS

You drew me from the womb,
    made me secure at my mother's breast.
I became Your charge at birth;
    from my mother's womb You have been my God.

Psalm 22:10–11 (Tanakh)

But I have calmed and quieted my soul,
like a weaned child with its mother;
my soul is like the weaned child that is with me.

Psalm 131:2

POEM

A MOTHER'S NATURE

I am closer to
nature than those
many hikes in mountain
and desert ever brought me. My child
curls at my bosom
with small foraging
movement, hands cupping
and finding what
belongs to her.
Her lips latching me,
a wellspring.
The let down begins.
I close my eyes
becoming a stream,
an apprentice of Mother Nature.
Balanced on a ritual
as old as origin,
we are interdependent,
little star and full moon.

Stacey Goldblatt

REFLECTION

Many Hindu mothers participate in a ritual of fasting and personal sacrifice as they symbolically release their sons to the world. This ritual is known as *phala ∂ana trata,* 'giving of her fruit to the world.'

BLESSING FOR WEANING

Judaism recognizes ceremonies and rituals for nearly every rite of passage, and included in the Torah are references to weaning celebrations. Since the process of weaning often happens over many months, this intimate blessing can take place whenever the mother feels it is time to observe this very personal life transition.

This blessing marks a separation between a mother and her child and celebrates the transformation of their relationship. The mother will likely choose to recognize the occasion privately, alone with her child. In the Jewish ceremony, someone other than the mother gives the first solid food to the child. Consider including this symbolic act to mark the occasion with your child and draw other family members into the experience.

PRAYER

You may wish to find a quiet spot to light a candle and nurse your child for the last time. It is very likely this will be a symbolic "last time" since the ultimate decision of when to stop nursing is often made by both the mother and the child, and it is important to build in this flexibility.

You may also wish to record some thoughts regarding this experience. You could include the date, the place, and your reflections about weaning your child. Close by reading the following blessing.

> Creator God,
> Today I come before you in thanksgiving
> for the partnership between us.
> Together we have created this child.
> In my womb you formed him.
> Within my womb I protected him.
> Into my arms you delivered him safely.
> In my arms I cradled him.
> In my body you created the food to sustain him.
> With my body I have fed him these many
>   months.
> And now, as he leaves the shelter of this first
>   love,
> hold and protect him in the years ahead.
>   Amen.

Lynn L. Caruso

BLESSING FROM MOTHER TO CHILD

[*insert child's name*],
From the moment of your birth I have cradled you to my breast. Nourished you with a love that was both a feast, yet more often a simple meal.

In some small way, remember these moments together. May you be blessed as you move out of my arms and into the circle of others. And may this experience of love continue to feed you all the days of your life.

Lynn L. Caruso

BLESSING FROM CHILD TO MOTHER

The child obviously will not be speaking these words of blessing, but just as the experience of nursing is one of reciprocity, so, too, is the act of blessing.

Lord God of the universe, You who created and brought forth all things, You have given us mothers who like Yourself bring forth life. Like You, our mother has nursed us, nurtured and tenderly cared over us. Feeding and clothing us, our mother has drawn us to her side giving us her very life. Grant that we should honor her and love her, to her benefit and Your glory.
Amen.

Robert E. Webber

REFLECTION

[In ancient times] the ebb and flow of the cycles within [women's] bodies made them watchful, mindful of the gifts of heaven and earth.

Anita Diamant, The New Jewish Baby Book

BENEDICTION

For everything there is a season,
and a time for every matter under heaven:

a time to be born, and a time to die;
a time to plant, and a time to pluck what is planted;
...
a time to embrace,
and a time to refrain from embracing....

Ecclesiastes 3:1–2, 5

5

Winter

A Season of Loss

With the coming of winter, the air chills and the dogwood outside my study gives up her final leaves. It is a season of darkness and loss. In this section, writers describe their losses — of mother or child — as being grounded in the season of winter. Gunilla Norris poignantly writes, "The killing frost has happened both in my garden and in my life. I have lost my mother." Many women describe this sense of feeling lost when their mothers died. The Zulu of Africa have a word to describe distance that the Jewish philosopher Martin Buber translates as "Where one cries, 'Mother, I am lost.'"

When my close friend was nearing the end of a devastating battle with breast cancer, her twelve-year-old daughter struggled with the gradual loss of her mother.

One evening while my friend was soaking in the bath-tub after a brutal round of chemotherapy, her daughter sat on the edge of the tub asking painful questions. Soon her daughter began sobbing and slid into the water, fully clothed, to cling to her mother. I imagine this young girl's heart rang with the cry, *Mother, I am lost!*

The "Winter" section begins with a look at the loss of history a woman experiences when she loses her mother. The second half honors the experience of losing children through miscarriage, war, illness, estrange-ment, and death. You will hear the pain in Maude Meehan's account of the severed relationship with her addicted son; and you will find hope in the words of Mirabai Starr, who writes that even though she suf-fered acutely when her teenage daughter died, she "was also being soothed and lifted by this ineffable holy joy."

I have witnessed five close friends suffer through the devastating loss of babies. The greatest pain I have ever seen is on the face of a mother who has just lost a small child. Walking beside my friend as she was wheeled out of the hospital without her infant son in her arms. Watching a nurse bind another friend's breasts to help her body stop preparing for mother-hood. Listening to yet another describe the wooden box that her father built to bury his granddaughter. Even though these babies were tiny, the size of each absence was immeasurable.

Each writer in this section has experienced a unique way of grieving and, ultimately, of healing. But many speak of the invaluable support they received from individuals who stood with them through the experience. Kathleen Finley describes this as "a wordless presence in faith." When we stand with a grieving mother, we validate the acute reality of her loss.

Each mother who has suffered the loss of a child will find herself at a different stage in the journey through grief. But, as Kathleen Finley writes, "Just as a woman who has had a child will always be a mom, so a woman who has lost a child will always be a bereaved mom."

Soon after my first son was born, a close childhood friend suffered the stillbirth of her own firstborn. I arrived at the hospital even before my friend woke from surgery, and, leaving my infant son in the waiting room with his grandfather, I walked in to find beautiful baby Grace being rocked in her grandmother's arms. I still remember the haunting scene: the darkened room, the rhythm of the rocking chair and, as the poet Rivage describes of her own experience, the only other sound was, "the keen, the high-pitched / whine my own ears sing in my head."

Later that night, as I carried my son out of the hospital, I was overcome with the realization that there is no greater love—and no greater loss—than that of a mother's. Yet even on the coldest winter days, we trust that spring will bring the thaw. Alongside the reflections on loss, this section includes words of hope from many faith traditions—hope that even in the shadow of loss, there is always the promise of light.

The killing frost has happened both in my garden and in my life. I have lost my mother. The harvest has been gathered. The light has changed. The new year is at hand.

Gunilla Norris, Journeying in Place

~

All is mortal.
Only the mother
is destined to immortality.
And when the mother
is no longer among the
living, she leaves a
memory which none yet
have dared to sully.
The memory of a mother
feeds a compassion in us
that is like the ocean —
and the illimitable ocean
feeds the rivers that dissect
the universe.

Isaac Babel

Say not in grief that she is no more
but say in thankfulness that she was.
A death is not the extinguishing of a light,
but the putting out of the lamp
because the dawn has come.

Rabindranath Tagore

For ever and for ever afterwards.
All, that doth live, lives always!
…
The end of birth is death; the end of death
Is birth: this is ordained!…
What is there sorrowful herein?

Bhagavad Gita, chapter 2, Of Doctrines

Enviable leaves,
Becoming
So beautiful
Just before falling ...

Masaoka Shiki

~

PRAYER AFTER SHIKI

Creator God,
who names the moment of our birth and death,
open our eyes to beauty in the midst of our loss.
And in these final days give me enduring strength
words of compassion, and the same selfless love
you have always shown.
Keep me present in the light of dusk.
The evening sun,
Becoming
So beautiful
Just before setting ...

Lynn L. Caruso

LETTING GO

Life and your fast approaching death
have stripped you of all passion,
all possessions, all amenities.
Even the desiccated husk
that houses pain and pride and gallant courage
fades and daily shrinks before my eyes.

Against translucent skin, white hair
gone thin as cobwebs clings
to your delineated skull, and I can see
the waning thread of blood move slowly
through a blue transparency of veins.

Crooning our old loved lulla-bye-bye song,
I gather up your crumpled frailty.
Daughter to mother, hold you, rock you outward
toward the tranquil, longed-for place.

Maude Meehan

It's happened
my mother doesn't know me —
first autumn rain

Winona L. Baker

~

BROODING GRIEF

A yellow leaf from the darkness
Hops like a frog before me.
Why should I start and stand still?

I was watching the woman that bore me
Stretched in the brindled darkness
Of the sick-room, rigid with will
To die: and the quick leaf tore me
Back to this rainy swill
Of leaves and lamps and traffic mingled before me.

D. H. Lawrence

~

For me, who go,
for you who stay behind
two autumns

Masaoka Shiki

I know now that I am mourning my mother through every season of the year. We all mourn this way. The first Christmas without the beloved, the first New Year. We will feel the loved one not here for the first bloom of forsythia, not here for the ripening of the pears, not here ... not here.

Gunilla Norris, Journeying in Place

Never does one feel oneself so utterly helpless as in trying to speak comfort for great bereavement. Time is the only comforter for the loss of a mother.

Jane Welsh Carlyle

It is impossible that something so natural, so universal, so necessary as death, should ever have been designed by God, as an evil.

Jonathan Swift

THE WALK

Last night I took a walk with him.
He tried to walk beyond his mother, I think.
We stood
in the mud beyond sidewalks, beyond this rim
of light that holds the city in, beyond
the church, beyond everything. You see,
I went to him to try to make him talk
about death. Half my life ago
my father died — his mother, yesterday.
Our opposite parents. I thought he would know
the way the child in him was pushed away,
the need to make a world when the first womb
is gone.
Creation — that's the point.

                                    And yet
he helped her die. Her eyes were shut.
She bled for weeks.
The doctors said she wouldn't make it
to Wednesday,
then to Friday. Finally he took her hand
and said, "Go to Daddy." While he walked away
to find a nurse, she understood.
She shut her hand
and died.
*Look at the snow blowing north
across the ground. It's cold tonight. We should
have worn our boots.*

                    Last night
it was as though he walked out of himself.
He said nothing. The way he walked said *misery*.
He took her misery so that she could go,
a kind of birth for her. But death for him.
He'll shut her in the ground. Is that birth?
Dead is dead.
                    And yet for him
pain seemed as natural as the notch
on that tree. For him bodies are the beginning
and the end and his only church
is his mind. He knows what animals know.
It was as though I watched the first man watch
his mother die. Remember that old hymn —
Miserere? Perhaps it's always been the sound
of blood pursuing blood, since the first dead,
through veins, through naves of muscle
        and around
the bruised, astonished altars of the head.

Well, tomorrow we'll send flowers. Yes, flowers.
But why can't I forget the way
        the darkness seemed
to gather in his marrow bones?
It seemed that in his eyes an old wind blew
        and sleet
freed stones. Old fires were built,
        old spears were hurled.

The pain of generations makes him complete.
He wouldn't talk. Perhaps he doesn't know.

But then why did it seem we were
    in another world
where the ground broke like water under our feet?

Jeanne Murray Walker

∽

The mother is everything—she is our consolation in sorrow, our hope in misery, and our strength in weakness. She is the source of love, mercy, sympathy, and forgiveness. He who loses his mother loses a pure soul who blesses and guards him constantly.

Kahlil Gibran, The Broken Wings

∽

In that place where there are no tears, nor death, nor sorrow, nor crying, nor pain, grant the joy of a new body and a new life for our loved one.
And in that place where there is no more night, give to [name] the light of Your countenance.

Robert E. Webber, Prayer of Commitment

AS IN BIRTH

For Hilary

My close friend and mother of three,
soaking in the bath last night after
a brutal round of chemotherapy,
told her daughter the truth,
and the young girl slid
into the warm water,
fully clothed — clinging
to her mother's breast
as in birth,
in death.

Rooting for something,
that would give her life.

Lynn L. Caruso

THE RED PEAR

For Devin

The red pear
sits on the pale tiled counter
silent and full

red as oxblood
as fresh sapped twigs.

I'd asked the young man in produce,
"Is it red inside?"
"I'm not sure," he confessed, then offered,
"I could find the manager. He'll know."

But I left him to his cloud of citrus —
stacking oranges, with
boxes to go.
"I'll wait till it ripens,
then I'll find out," I said.

My eyes cherish its shape in my kitchen.
The phone screams like a jay.
My sister. Her grandson,
due in three weeks,
has died.

I see his mother, only eighteen,
with my nephew beside her in a hospital
room, the clatter of carts in the hall
drowned by the absence of her infant's cry.

After they induced her to labor
his small
lifeless body from hers
was she able to hold him?
What did she say for good-bye?
Did my nephew echo
her words in the hollowed
voice of a man?

I allow the flesh of their grief
to stay hidden. I do not ask.
My ears gather instead the thousands of miles
of silence my sister needs to speak.
When we are done, the black phone back
in its nest, I cup the red pear in my hands.

I close my eyes and sway, gently
shifting my weight. The old dog comes and
leans against me, holds me to the day
with his presence and his labored breath.

The only other sound is the keen, the high-pitched
whine my own ears sing in my head.
The cradled pear, smooth skin morning cool
against mine, gives me its firm full weight.

I stand and wait for the pear to ripen.
I try to dream what color it will be.

Rivage

~

Do not give up ... When you first begin, you find only
darkness, and as it were a cloud of unknowing. You
don't know what this means except that in your will you
feel a simple steadfast intention reaching out towards
God ... Reconcile yourself to wait in this darkness as
long as is necessary, but still go on longing after him
whom you love.

The Cloud of Unknowing

~

With the death of a parent there is a loss of history, but
with the death of a child the loss is of future hopes and
dreams. It's a place where words fail us, and the only
consolation is a wordless presence in faith and holding
one another.

Kathleen Finley, The Liturgy of Motherhood

ST. KEVIN'S BLACKBIRD

Outstretched in Lent, St. Kevin's hands
did not expect
the blackbird's egg. Think prayer

as nest—an intimate travail wherein
all things fledging leave behind
a kind of grave. *Amen* seemed

premature, so faith-in-waiting
incubated. Afterward,
did he save those eggshell bits,

arrange a fragile
rosary with each goodbye
the smallest beak ever made?

He never said. Nor will he
know this mother's heart, mourning you,
more shell than shelter. May it

fissure, let in light enough
for me to murmur: Yes, let grief be,
with every loss, a readied womb.

                              Laurie Klein

IN FLIGHT

We rock
above glacial clouds
carving grief lines
on sky.

One could fall through.

Below, the plains shamelessly scatter
their deck. Canyons wrinkle skin
that the rivers have shed.

Tomorrow
you would have been
three months
learning my face.

Now loss has me
on a leash. I race
between homes
with a faint lantern

my body
a chasm within which
your heartbeat continues
to continue

to disappear.

Amy Klauke Minato

Isabel was born at seven in the morning. I recognized my child in her face in an instant; she looked just like her brothers. With so little body fat, she had the appearance of a wise old woman. Her heart rate was slow. Her lungs were too sticky to allow air into them. She could not take a full breath on her own and no one forced her to do so. No one did anything to her that caused her pain or discomfort. Instead, she nestled in Charlie's arms, feeling his breathing, listening to his heartbeat, while hers slowed, then ceased. We gave her back to God.

Isabel did not need length of years to be the person she was meant to be. She allowed us to love her as our daughter. We did our best to give her peace in return. Her life may have been short, but it was full.

The trees on the hill where we buried Isabel were as empty of leaves as those in my yard. The rain of Thanksgiving had turned into snow, and a light dusting of white illuminated the intricate perfection of large branches supporting smaller branches, then even smaller, graceful branches generating the tiniest of twigs. Seeing the tree empty this way, I realized its beauty came from the branches' varying lengths; it was the inequality of its parts that made it complete. Isabel was not a medical miracle. She was the tiny branch without whom our family would be incomplete. Isabel was a moment of grace.

Mary Douthitt, "A Moment of Grace"

AFTER A MISCARRIAGE

God of all life, how can this be?
How can you take away this little one
before he or she even had a chance to live?
In faith I know that this creation of yours is with
    you now,
but I ask for some peace in the midst of my pain
and numbness.

And what is it that you have in mind for me,
as I am left disappointed and without this child,
a little one that I was beginning to prepare to
    welcome?
Help me to know that you have something
even better in mind for me,
even when I can't imagine it now.

Please bless all those who have lost a child —
either before or after birth;
be with them in their grief and pain,
in their questions and their anger.

Help us to know that you are there
to hold us and to weep with us,
and help us to remember that in your
    Resurrection
there is always life from death.

Help me to listen for your voice in my life
and to know your deep care and peace
as I give this unborn child into your loving arms.
Amen.

Kathleen Finley

Gracious God,
We lift up this child, still swaddled
in our hopes and dreams for her.
Comfort us in our mourning.
And into this place of brokenness
pour your light of peace. Amen.

Lynn L. Caruso

BIRTHS AND DEATHS

Our baby was will be has been born every May
a fetching little girl
with your blonde hair, my brown eyes.
No, your blue eyes, your curls
laughter, passion, all yours.
A work in progress.
She has been growing clever
sweet enough to eat.
She flies from us in shrieks, giggles.
Nightly we share her toes, collective kisses.

Today, in fall's drear, you announce
your wife's pregnancy, due in May.
Our child, arms out-stretched, lips parted,
    dissolves too
quickly for a snatched hug,
    even a wave bye-bye.
I grasp but she's gone.
Mere adjective, two-dimensional,
pinned on this wintry page.
Ephemeral or faery.
A cunning specimen fixed.

Aglow with imminent fatherhood
fluttering death passes beyond you.
My lap is heart hollow.

Come May, season of green re-awakenings
from her aerie
    our watchful little daughter will glide
      through the delivery room
        one of your most rare sightings
          to warble a bliss song on the birth
      of her half-sibling
    who will make her

            Whole.

            Crystal Hurdle

~

Just as a woman who has had a child will always be a mom, so a woman who has lost a child will always be a bereaved mom.

    Kathleen Finley, The Liturgy of Motherhood

They that love beyond the world cannot be separated by it. Death is but crossing the world, as friends do the seas; they live in one another still.

William Penn

~

PRAYER ON THE LOSS OF AN UNBORN CHILD

For Sara, Jill, Krisi, and Amy

Creator God,
The one who knew all our days
when none of them as yet existed,
comfort this mother in her loss.
The child, held only in her womb,
is loved beyond this world.

Today she stands on grief's shore
the sea rolls out before her in dark waves.
Sustain her with the promise
that you are waiting on the other side.

Surround her with family and friends
to hold her in this absence.
And let them christen her, *mother*,
for all the months the child lived,
for all the days she'll walk alone.

Creator God,
though you now cradle her child in your arms,
comfort this mother with the knowledge that
"they live in one another still." Amen.

Lynn L. Caruso

~

I was not aware of the moment when I first crossed
the threshold of this life ...

When in the morning I looked upon the light, I felt
in a moment that I was no stranger in this world, that
the inscrutable without name and form had taken me
in its arms in the form of my own mother.

Even so, in death the same unknown will appear
as ever known to me. And because I love this life, I
know I shall love death as well.

The child cries out when from the right breast the
mother takes it away, in the very next moment to find
in the left one its consolation.

Rabindranath Tagore, Gitanjali

STILL BIRTH

You were there,
weren't you?
Just yesterday I felt you turn
inside me, and today
nothing.

On the screen your heart
has stopped beating.
The technician says, "I'm sorry,"
and my heart
beats faster.

What happened between
yesterday and today,
between the rise and
fall of our tummies.
Now only mine
falling.

Four pounds is large
enough. I count like I'm
supposed to—ten
fingers, ten toes.

Who decides who stays
or leaves and why does
anyone, especially you,
have to go now, leaving
this and all of me
behind?

Sarah K. Bain

~

In response to the loss of two friends' babies

[They left behind a] message of the existence of love,
a love whose size can be measured by the size of the
pain that it leaves behind.

Margaret Hebblethwaite, Motherhood and God

~

Naked you came
from Earth the Mother.
Naked you return to her.
May a good wind be your road.

Omaha prayer

In May of 1998 our 25-year-old daughter, Krista
Hunt Ausland, lay dying in a remote Andean ravine. In
one midnight moment, she and our son-in law, Aaron
Ausland, were resting peacefully in a microbus, holding
hands as their puppy Choclo snuggled on their laps. In
the next terror filled moment, their speeding microbus
plunged over a cliff, tossing passengers out the win-
dows like rag dolls.   It was August when we began
the pilgrimage to the land of our daughter's last days.

...

Two crosses covered with gaudy plastic flowers
marked the site. The bus had recently been removed
and now a long swath through the dense brush scarred
the mountainside....

When we neared the bottom where the bus landed,
Aaron showed us the place he remembered first seeing
Krista's body. "She was the last thrown from the bus,"
he said as he tried to reconstruct his memories.

I placed the flowers where Aaron thought she
died, a gesture that felt completely unsatisfying. Then
Jim and I sat side by side, confronting the unimaginable truth that our beloved daughter breathed her last
breath in this Andean ravine, so far from home.

Questions surfaced in the heat. I wondered if she
was conscious during those last few minutes of life,
alone before Aaron could find her and hold her? Did
her eyes see the stars of heaven, so abundant in

Bolivia's nights? I thought of Aaron's trusting prayer for safety shortly after the bus left Comarapa, a natural expression of his intimate relationship with God, and the theological questions her death ushered into his life, scarred already with the recent loss of his mother to breast cancer.

I cried for her, for all the days of lost love; for Aaron's bewildering pain; for the unborn children no one will ever know; for Susan and Jeff, a sister and brother who will lose a lifetime of familial friendship; for Jim, whose father's heart broke into as many shards as the shattered bus. And I cried a mother's tears, for the child I first knew in the womb, whose light illumined every day of our family's life and filled my own with such joy.

I remember thinking, "I'm not going to try to understand it. It makes no human sense that a woman of Krista's spirit and heart and love that wants to give to the world ... " to see her killed. There's no way to understand it.... My hope is that we could be open to God's grace, God's mercy, knowing that God stays alongside us whatever life brings.

Linda Lawrence Hunt, "A Terrible Beauty"

FROM PIECES

For Linda, in memory of your daughter
Krista Hunt Ausland

Ancient Japanese monks once kept ceramic cups as
one of their few possessions. It has been told that, cen-
turies later when one of these cups was dropped, shat-
tering to the floor, it was not discarded but was instead
repaired with gold solder. The repair made the break
more prominent but also gave the cup a new beauty.

When the call came that your daughter had died.
That the bus left the road and fell to the valley floor
below. That her husband searched the Bolivian
hillside to find her in the black night.
Then walked on alone.

Your cup slipped. Shattered.

When you buried her beside a statue of St. Francis,
beneath stories of love and life lived richly.
Mourning the daughter you had known
in your womb. Feeling, again, those first kicks.
When the dogwood bloomed that spring
and you realized great loss lives in the same
house as great love.

You knelt to gather the pieces.

When you traveled to her home in that mountain
   village, and hiked to the ravine where she died.

Setting flowers on the scar carved deep
into the earth by the falling bus. Knowing
this would be a wound that would always show.
When you knelt where her body might have lain
and wondered what she last saw — the sky
of stars, her husband's wild eyes, black night?

You worked to match the shards.

When you met the old woman who took your place
to dress your daughter's broken body.
Spraying her mud home for scorpions
as villagers came weaving their stories of your
daughter's love for the cooperative,
for the children, for the God of tarantulas.
When you knew that she would choose to live on.

You warmed the gold solder. Poured it in the
      open places.

When you returned home to find the grief was so
deep it held you to your bed and your keen rang on.
When you finally stood and said,
I'm not going to try to understand it,
then filled the hillside behind your house
with peonies and cherry trees
and found that with your hands
      you could make things live.

You held the pieces till the solder cooled.

When you started a library, and a foundation that
sent out others in her name.
When you learned that burrowing into the grief
that buried you, there was a spring called love.
And it was deep. And it would never dry up.
And drinking of it gave you life.

You rose and passed the cup.

Lynn L. Caruso

~

There's acute grief for the first one or two years that
ebbs for most people. [But for parents] sorrow will go
with you to your grave. It's just so huge. But enormous
loss is related to enormous love.... In time, I discovered
that underlying a parent's deep grief is a vast reservoir
of love. If you can tap that, you actually access a rich
resource of healing and creative energy because love is
powerful and enduring love never ends.

Linda Lawrence Hunt

*Please see "Editor's Note" on page 242 for more information about
The Krista Foundation.*

RIDE

Always saddled, grief
canters alongside, by turns
strident, furtive,
winsome. You called me Mom,
and I, who'd raised
daughters, held out

a heart you pocketed. Moving on
without a goodbye — that was the first
loss. Then the body bag, a silent
captain zipping you in,
keeping vigil. I would have, too. Until
anguish slips off its spurs,

I erase all but your arms:
    hefting my groceries,
waltzing our 80-pound mutt,
bringing roses. This is how
to forestall grief, until I can
leap, straddle it bareback.

Laurie Klein

SIX A.M. PHONE CALL

Your voice rips sleep away,
disintegrates
three thousand miles
six months
of false reprieve.

Hand tense on the receiver
I will myself not to receive
the hunger in your voice.
Force myself to recall
friends, lovers,
family you left.
Returning now and then
to feast on us and leave.

Your travels now
are circumscribed,
from cell to ward
to street and back again.
Only your counselor remains
and you complain she feeds you
Thorazine instead of words.
I cannot nourish you,
I know that now.
This cupboard's stripped
of all but pain.

You're right; there's no one left,
no, nothing more to say.
The vacant hum of wire swallows you
as you did us, with mindless
impervious detachment. Aching
I place the phone back gently
in its cradle. Lost man,
I cannot do the same for you.

Maude Meehan

~

LAMENT OF MARY FOR HER SON

I am overwhelmed, O my son,
I am overwhelmed by love
And I cannot endure
That I should be in the chamber
And you on the wood of a cross
I in the house
And you in the tomb.

Anonymous Syrian woman

Soon after September 11, 2001, my fourteen-year-old daughter Jenny was killed in a car accident. In that moment, the global grief I had been witnessing at a distance became intensely personal for me. I shared the pain of every mother everywhere—American, Afghani, Iraqi—as she struggled to bear the unbearable.

For a year, or more, all I could do was tentatively face the fire of my feelings, offer quiet prayers for peace on the planet and in the hearts of all who were grieving. I sat amid the wreckage of my own heart, allowing the shattered fragments to reform according to the inscrutable timetable of the Divine, relinquishing any last illusion that I had control of anything in this life.

Eventually, like so many victims of tragedy, I turned my attention to service. This was the only path that made any sense.

...

The death of a child is every parent's worst nightmare come true.... The loss of such potential, coupled with the primal agony of missing her, threatened to destroy me.

But there was another reality just beyond the edges of my anguish. A palpable sense of holiness began to pervade the emptiness carved by my shattering. As my family and community rallied to support me in those first hours and days of my loss, filling the air with their prayers and tears and singing, I noticed a radiance wash over my heart and the hearts of my circle of support. God was with us. And Jenny was with God. The exaltation accompanying this phenomenon confused me. The most terrible thing imaginable had happened and, while my suffering was acute, I was also being soothed and lifted by this ineffable holy joy.

Mirabai Starr, "Shepherds in the Night"

Deep peace of the running wave to you;
Deep peace of the flowing air to you;
Deep peace of the quiet earth to you;
Deep peace of the shining stars to you;
Deep peace of the gentle night to you;
Moon and stars pour their healing light on you.

Celtic prayer

ELEGY

I am going home with thee
To thy home! To thy home!
I am going home with thee
To thy home of winter.
I am going home with thee
To thy home! To thy home!
I am going home with thee
To thy home of autumn,
of spring and of summer.

I am going home with thee,
Thou child of my love,
To thine eternal bed
To thy perpetual sleep.

Gaelic hymn

~

Warm summer sun, shine kindly here;
Warm western wind, blow softly here;
Green sod above, lie light, lie light —
Good-night, dear heart, good-night, good-night.

Robert Richardson, adapted by Mark Twain

6

The Divine Mother
A Sustaining Taproot

While the previous sections have celebrated human mothers, this section looks to the Maternal Divine as the archetype of motherhood and a model for our parenting. We inherit most of our knowledge of motherhood from our own mothers, but even the strongest maternal roots are limited in the amount of sustenance they can offer. Yet, as a taproot that provides anchor in strong winds and nourishment from the deepest buried source, the Divine Mother sustains us with a renewing wellspring of comfort, strength, and wisdom. "As the mother nourishes the body," writes George William Russell, "so the Mighty Mother nourishes the soul."

While pregnant with my first child, I was hospital-ized with preterm labor and then spent more than three months on bed rest at home. My days in the hospital were filled with medications to stop the contractions, numerous tests, and overwhelming anxiety: Could I somehow have prevented this? Would our baby be born premature? If so, would he be healthy? My mother flew nearly three thousand miles to sit beside me in that darkened hospital room, to just "be present" in the uncertainty.

Recalling a passage from Psalm 139, she assured me that, even though my child was still unknown to us, he was already fully known and "wonderfully made" by his Creator—a Creator who not only knew the day of my child's birth, but all the days that were formed for him, "when none of them as yet existed." These words remained with me for the rest of my pregnancy, bringing great peace and helping me to relinquish some of my anxiety, trusting that my child was already being protected, loved, held, and *mothered* by his Creator.

Although many of us have been raised with the view of God as Father, God is not universally viewed as masculine. This section includes maternal motifs drawn from many faith traditions: being cradled in Kali's arms and sustained by Mother Earth; the Tao giving birth to all creation; God protecting us like a mother hen. Exploring images of the Divine Mother in a variety of faith traditions can inform and enrich our mothering.

The worship of maternal deities preceded paternal ones, and many believe the archetype of the Maternal Divine had its beginnings in a goddess of Paleolithic times. For ancient religions, Mother God was closely related to Mother Earth or Mother Nature. These religions worshiped the earth as the source of life and the fertile mother of all things. For subsistence cultures, who lived close to the land, it's not surprising that they drew a connection between a god who created the world and a woman who creates and gives birth to a child. In the Hindu tradition, the goddess Devi is viewed as the very soil of life.

The one quality of the Divine that resonates throughout the faith traditions represented in this section is that God is love, in all its varied forms. The very qualities that *Honoring Motherhood* celebrates — a mother's tenderness, provision, forgiveness, and sacrifice — are the qualities of God's love for us.

This unfailing love is the core of the mother-child relationship — even if some days are about repairing that fractured love. As Sarah Napthali's piece in the "Summer" section so poignantly stated, "My daughter has taken me to hell and back but there's nothing she can do to make me stop loving her." Strikingly similar is the prayer by Sikh writer Arjan: "Even if I have gone astray, I am thy child, O God; thou art my father and mother."

The Creator explored by writers in this section is not distant. She desires intimate connection and relationship. She mothers beside us and knows what we endure. She is a God who understands the depth of our work and mothers us, as we mother our own children.

THANKS TO MOTHER EARTH

Onen, we give thanks
To our mother, the Earth,
For she gives us all that we need for life.

She supports our feet
As we walk upon her.
She is there to catch us
If we should fall.

It has always been this way
Since the beginning,
For she is our mother,
The one who cares for us.

It gives us great joy
That Mother Earth
Continues still to care for us.

So it is that we join
Our minds together
To give greetings and thanks
To the Earth, our mother.

Mohawk, eastern woodlands

I sing to the Mother Gaia.
I sing to the Father Sun.
I sing to the living in the garden where
The Mother and the Father are One.

Anonymous

~

I will sing of the well-founded Earth,
Mother of all, eldest of all beings.
She feeds all creatures that are in the world,
all that go upon the goodly land,
and all that are in the paths of the seas,
and all that fly: all these are fed of her store.

Hail, Mother of the gods, wife of starry Heaven;
freely bestow upon me for this my song
substance that cheers the heart!

Homeris Hymns XXX

Earth our mother, breathe forth life
all night sleeping
now awaking
in the east
now see the dawn

Earth our mother, breathe and waken
leaves are stirring
all things moving
new day coming
life renewing

Eagle soaring, see the morning
see the new mysterious morning
something marvelous and sacred
though it happens every day
Dawn the child of God and Darkness

Pawnee prayer

~

Holy Mother Earth, the trees
and all nature are witnesses of
your thoughts and deeds.

Winnebago saying

The earth is your mother,
   she holds you.
The sky is your father,
   he protects you.
We are together always.
We are together always.
There never was a time
   when this
   was not so.

Navajo lullaby

~

Everything in nature bespeaks the mother. The sun is the mother of earth and gives it its nourishment of heat; it never leaves the universe at night until it has put the earth to sleep to the song of the sea and the hymn of birds and brooks. And this earth is the mother of trees and flowers. It produces them, nurses them, and weans them. The trees and flowers become kind mothers of their great fruits and seeds. And the mother, the prototype of all existence, is the eternal spirit, full of beauty and love.

Kahlil Gibran, The Broken Wings

The Great Spirit is our father, but the earth is our mother. She nourishes us; that which we put into the ground she returns to us, and healing plants she gives us likewise. If we are wounded, we go to our mother and seek to lay the wounded part against her, to be healed. Animals too, do thus, they lay their wounds to the earth.

Big Thunder, Wabanakis Nation

Mother Earth lies in the world's midst
rounded like an egg and all Blessings are there
inside her as in a honeycomb.

Petronius, first-century Roman

I am the womb of every womb; I am the seed producing every form of existence.

The Song of God 14:4

We have passed you on your roads.
Here for you we leave these seeds.
When in the spring,
Your earth mother is wet,
In your earth mother
You will bury these seeds.
Carefully they will bring forth their young.

Zuni, Native American Pueblo people

~

The Mother of Songs, the mother of our whole seed, bore us in the beginning. She is the mother of all races and the mother of all tribes. She is the mother of the thunder, the mother of the rivers, the mother of the trees and all kinds of things. She is the mother of songs and dances. She is the mother of the stones. She is the mother of the dance paraphernalia and of all temples and the only mother we have. She is the mother of animals, the only one, and the mother of the Milky Way. She is the mother of the rain, the only one we have. She alone is the mother of things, she alone.

Kagaba, South American Indians

HYMNS TO THE GODDESS (DEVI)

O Mother of the world, O Mother!
I have not worshipped Thy feet,
Nor have I given abundant wealth to Thee;
Yet the affection which Thou bestoweth on me
    is without compare,
For a bad son may sometimes be born,
    but a bad mother never.
For children afflicted by hunger and thirst
    ever remember their mother.
O Mother of the world!

John Woodroffe (pseudonym for Arthur Avalon)

~

HYMN TO THE MOTHER OF THE GODS

Hail to our mother, who caused the yellow flowers to blossom, who scattered the seeds of the maguey, as she came forth from Paradise.... Hail to the goddess who shines in the thorn bush like a bright butterfly. Ho! She is our mother, goddess of the earth.

Rig Veda Americanus:
Sacred Songs of the Ancient Mexicans

HYMN TO GODDESS EARTH

Into thy middle set us, O earth, and into thy navel, into the nourishing strength that has grown from thy body; purify thyself for us! The earth is the mother, and I the son of the earth;

...

Thy summer, O earth, thy rainy season, thy autumn, winter, early spring, and spring; thy decreed yearly seasons, thy days and nights shall yield us milk.

Gentle, fragrant, kindly ... rich in milk, the broad earth together with (her) milk shall give us courage!

Hymns of the Atharva-Veda: 12, 36, 59

~

O Evening Star, thou bringest all that's best:
The sheep, the goat, thou bringest home, to rest:
The child thou bringest to the mother's breast.

Sappho

The calm sea is the Absolute; the same sea in waves is Divine Mother. She is time, space, and causation. God is Mother and has two natures, the conditioned and the unconditioned. As the former, She is God, nature, and soul (humanity). As the latter, She is unknown and unknowable. Out of the Unconditioned came the trinity god, nature, and soul, the triangle of existence.... A bit of Mother, a drop, was Krishna, another was Buddha, another was Christ. The worship of even one spark of Mother in our earthly mother leads to greatness. Worship Her if you want love and wisdom.

Swami Vivekananda

~

The Divinity is attentive to us like a nursing mother with a child, who keeps his feeding schedule, who knows when he will be weaned, and how long he will grow with milk, and how long he will be nourished with bread. And She weighs him and gives him more food according to the state of his development.

Saint Ephrem, Hymns of the Church

As a mother comforts her son
So I will comfort you.

Isaiah 66:13 (Tanakh)

⁓

Lord, how glad we are that we don't hold you
but that you hold us.

Haitian prayer

⁓

While the child is still in its mother's arms it is nourished by her, yet it does not know it is a mother which
feeds it. It knows later in whose bosom it has lain. As
the mother nourishes the body, so the Mighty Mother
nourishes the soul.

George William Russell, The Candle of Vision

⁓

My Lord God, my All in all, Life of my life, and Spirit
of my spirit ... the hunger and the thirst of this heart of
mine can be satisfied only with thee who has given
birth. O Creator mine!

Sadhu Sundar Singh, At the Master's Feet

On January 7 of this year, I crossed over into a new world—and my life changed forever. On that brisk winter morning I labored and cried out as I became the mother of a beautiful baby boy.... Since he was born—really, since conception—he has had nothing to eat but what has come from my body. I know, I'm getting a little personal here—but it constantly amazes me that from my very self, my very being, this little person is nourished.

It is a lot of work to be a mother. It is wonderful to be a mother, but it is a lot of work. When Moses was leading the people of Israel through the desert, he likened his job to that of being a mother—and he said he didn't want that job any more. He said, in fact, that he *would rather die* than nurse and carry these people into the promised land. It was as if he said, "You're gonna have to do it, God, 'cause this job's too big for me."

Indeed, God did exactly that. Every morning manna fell to the ground and fed the people. Every day the cloud traveled with them and protected them. From their first day in the wilderness to their last, God provided for their every need. Just as an infant neither works to provide for its own food or its safety, so the infant nation of Israel had only to receive from the God who held and fed them.

Rev. Susie Crawford Beil, from her sermon
"The God Who Feeds"

NOW PLEASE BRING YOUR SMALL CHILD HOME

O Kali, the drama of my life
    was composed and acted out
in the blazing summer field of destiny.

Now please bring Your small child home
    through the fragrant cool of evening,
cradled in Your arms, lost in Your gaze,
    disappearing in Your love.

Ramprasad Sen

~

The soul that worships becomes always a little child; the
soul that becomes a child finds God oftenest as mother.

Sister Nivedita, Kali the Mother

~

My child, you need not know much in order to please
Me. Only love Me dearly. Speak to Me, as you would
talk to your mother, if she had taken you in her arms.

Sister Nivedita, Kali the Mother

Editor's Note: Kali is a central figure in late medieval Bengali devotional literature.

IF YOU WANT

If you want,
the Virgin will come walking down the road
pregnant with the holy,
and say,

"I need shelter for the night,
please take me inside your heart,
my time is so close."

Then, under the roof of your soul,
you will witness the sublime
intimacy, the divine, the Christ
taking birth
forever,

as she grasps your hand for help, for each of us
is the midwife of God, each of us.
Yes there, under the dome of your being
does Creation come into existence eternally
through your womb, dear pilgrim—
the sacred womb in your soul,

as God grasps our arms for help;
for each of us is
his beloved servant
never
far.

If you want,
the Virgin will come walking
down the street pregnant
with Light and
sing.

Saint John of the Cross

~

You look upon us with the love of a mother for
her children.

Hymns of the Atharva-Veda

~

DIVINE BLESSING

Almighty Lord, giver of all blessings,
You watch over us "with the love of a mother
for her children."

In every lullaby, and first step,
every night of fever and day of brokenness,
your spirit dwells. Open our eyes to your presence,
bathing us with the knowledge that you
are the bringer of all blessings.

Lynn L. Caruso

HYMN TO THE BLESSED VIRGIN

O my Lady, the holy Virgin Mary, thou hast been likened to many things, yet there is nothing which compares with thee. Neither heaven can match thee, nor the earth equal as much as the measure of thy womb. For thou didst confine the Unconfinable, and carry him whom none has power to sustain.

...

The Virgin's womb was the ark and dwelling-place of the Lord God Adonay.... Honour to her who bore thee; homage to her who gave birth to thee, devotion to thy mother; and holiness to her who tended thee.

Ethiopian Orthodox hymn

Hail, star causing the Sun to shine:
Hail, womb of the divine Incarnation.
Hail, for through thee
    the creation is made new:
Hail, for through thee
    the Creator becomes a newborn child.

Akathist Orthodox hymn

BLESSED VIRGIN COMPARED
TO THE AIR WE BREATHE

Wild air, world-mothering air,
Nestling me everywhere,
...
This needful, never spent,
And nursing element;
My more than meat and drink,
My meal at every wink;
This air, which, by life's law,
My lung must draw and draw
Now but to breathe its praise,
Minds me in many ways
Of her who not only
Gave God's infinity
Dwindled to infancy
Welcome in womb and breast,
Birth, milk, and all the rest
But mothers each new grace
That does now reach our race—
Mary Immaculate.

Gerard Manley Hopkins

The Tao gives birth to all of creation.
The virtue of Tao in nature nurtures them,
and their family gives them their form.
Their environment then shapes them into
    completion.
That is why every creature honors the Tao and its
    virtue.
...
It gives them life without wanting to possess them,
and cares for them expecting nothing in return.
It is their master, but it does not seek to dominate
    them.
This is called the dark and mysterious virtue.

Lao-Tzu, Tao Te Ching

~

Who is my mother? Who is my father?
    Only you, O God.
You watch me, guard me, on every path,
    through every darkness.

Kekchi Maya people of Guatemala

~

Even if I have gone astray, I am thy child, O God;
thou art my father and mother.

Sikh master guru Arjan Dev

As a child that hath lost his mother,
So am I troubled, my heart is seared with sore
    anguish:
O merciful God,
Thou knowest my need,
Come, save me, and show me Thy love.

Tukaram, Indian peasant mystic, 1608

~

We need to be able to let those tears go and that bitterness dissolve and find that, after all, maternity is not destroyed, because it is on our [M]other's breast that we have been weeping. God will understand all, forgive all, share with us in all, and her tenderness will never crack, nor her imagination fail. In her there will always be new springs of eternal love, that we can always draw from, so long as we turn to them as a child, accepting our human shortcoming and not rejecting her divine limitlessness.

Margaret Hebblethwaite, Motherhood and God

[God cared for Jacob ...]
As an eagle stirs up its nest,
and hovers over its young;
as it spreads its wings, takes them up,
and bears them aloft on its pinions,
the Lord ... nursed him with honey from the crags
... and milk from the flock.

Deuteronomy 32:11, 13, 14

~

How often have I desired to gather your children
together as a hen gathers her brood under her wings.

Luke 13:34

~

Thou art the Father and Mother of the Universe,
moving and unmoving;
the end of all its worship;
greater than the greatest —
there is none to equal Thee
in sea, earth or sky ...
O God of gods, Nest of the universe!

The Song of God 11:43, 45

7

Sowing the Seeds
The Power of a Mother's Love

The closing section of *Honoring Motherhood* moves beyond the intimate mother-child dyad—tending to our own garden—to explore the implications of loving our world with the love cultivated in motherhood: *sowing the seeds*.

The Tibetan lama Sogyal Rinpoche teaches that the path of compassion starts with returning to the memories of our childhood when we were "loved genuinely once." When we love our children selflessly, we become the catalyst for such compassion, the givers of this genuine love. As our children learn through our example how to love others, they will sow the seeds of compassion even wider. Just as the natural world perpetuates itself through the seasons, we can nurture our children to become the next generation of sowers.

In the "Winter" section of this book, I included the story of my friend Linda, whose daughter was tragically killed in a bus accident while serving with the Mennonite Central Committee in Bolivia. After months of mourning, this mother found the strength to channel her grief and her mother-love into her life's work. She created The Krista Foundation in honor of her daughter, to support young people engaged in service work throughout the world. In her daughter's absence, Linda has sown her seeds of enduring love out into the greater world.

As mothers, our days are filled with the ordinary demands of caring for our children, and it is often difficult to see our impact on the "greater world." But as Rev. Gina Hilton-VanOsdall reflects, this mundane work is, in essence, about feeding the hungry and clothing the naked, and she resolves to "attend to each task with attention and compassion, / As if the redemption of the whole world depended on it."

Motherhood helps us learn selfless giving, tolerance for difference, unconditional love, fierce protectiveness, devotion, and service — qualities that prepare us for the work of compassion and justice. In time, many mothers make an intentional choice to direct the love for their child beyond their own four walls, outward to include the greater world.

Our hearts, which were initially stretched open by an overpowering love for our child in those first days of motherhood, are broken further by witnessing the world's pain and suffering. The news headlines become almost unbearable as we are acutely aware that the horrors of war, crime, and addiction leave broken families and suffering mothers in their wake. Writer Jacqueline Kramer describes "the spiritually conscious mother [as one who] sees behind the masks of differences into the heart of sameness ... all beings become her children." What begins as a desire to heal the world for the sake of our own children ripens into something more.

Throughout the world, mothers are politically fueled by this recognition of "sameness." While traveling in Guatemala, I met with representatives of the *Grupo de Apoyo Mutuo* (GAM) a "Group of Mutual Support" for mothers of the disappeared. Through decades of civil war, their suffering has united them to seek justice not just for their own missing kin but for all who have disappeared.

We are all loved with the same Divine Mother love, and this kinship has great implications for how we approach our world. I cannot look into the face of my First World baby and say, "You are God's favorite." In fact, there are many who believe the opposite—that God cradles all Third World infants and soothes them with the same words: "You are my favorite." As mothers, we don't nurse one child and leave the other to starve. It is the same with our Divine Parent. We demand love and justice in our home; God demands love and justice in the world.

The purest love does not expect a return of that love. With an enduring constancy, the sun gives life season after season. And many of the writers in this collection would agree: that is the nature, and the power, of a mother's love.

Living with *loving kindness, compassion, sympathetic joy* and *equanimity* would happen quite naturally if we could sense our interconnectedness with others.... As mothers we serve our children as though they are parts of ourselves: their comfort is our comfort. The challenge is to bring this kind of love and compassion to all our relationships until nobody is excluded.

Sarah Napthali, Buddhism for Mothers

～

Oh what a power is motherhood,
Possessing a potent spell
All women alike
Fight fiercely for a child.

Euripides

We thank you for that love which will not stay its hold till it joins all nations and kindreds and tongues and people into one great family of love.

Theodore Parker

~

God, we pray, not simply for the health and well-being of those gathered around our table, but for those gathered around tables everywhere.

We pray, not only for the peace and security of our neighborhoods, but for neighborhoods scattered across the globe.

We pray, not merely for quality education and opportunity for our own children, but for all children. For we are your people. We belong to your family. All your children are indeed our own.

Rev. Gina Hilton-VanOsdall

TONGLEN FOR MOTHERS

*Tonglen is a traditional Buddhist practice of compassion.
In order to have compassion for ourselves, we cultivate it
for others. We take in the difficult parts of mothering,
for ourselves and for all mothers and send out compassion and love.*

> I breathe in the daily frustrations
>   small as they are, big as they can seem
> I breathe out patience for us all.
>
> I breathe in the loneliness
>   of days spent mothering on our own
> I breathe out connection
>   community, compassion.
>
> I breathe in the brokenness
>   not being enough in the world
> I breathe out wholeness
>   leaving ideals behind, truth.
>
> I breathe in the boredom
>   diapers, cooking, same every day
> I breathe out simple pleasure
>   swings, finger painting, rocks.

I breathe in the exhaustion,
   the worry, the fear
I breathe out calm energy, excitement.

I breathe in the rage
   at your plight, your place, your life
I breathe out peace
   contentment, courage.

DeLona Campos-Davis

I WRITE OF THAT JOURNEY

I remember how my mother would hold me.
I would look up at her sometimes
and see her weep.

I understand now what was happening.
Love so strong a force
it broke the
cage,

and she disappeared from everything
for a blessed
moment.

All actions have evolved
from the taste of flight;
the hope of freedom
moves our cells
and limbs.

Unable to live on the earth,
Mira ventured out alone in the sky,
I write of that journey
of becoming as
free as
God.

Don't forget love;
it will bring all the madness you need
to unfurl yourself across
the universe.

Mirabai, sixteenth-century Hindu mystical poetess

As we recall the compassion shown us by our parents, so may we dedicate ourselves to turning that compassion towards all the inhabitants of the earth.

Yom Kippur prayer

O God, the Father of all, we commend to your ceaseless compassion all homeless children and orphans and those whose lives are overshadowed by violence or thwarted by disease or cruelty. Awaken in us your living charity that we may not rest while children cry for bread or go uncomforted for lack of love.

Author unknown

NURSING FINN

Six times a day
for the past ten months,
in the rocker, on the sofa,
in lawnchairs on the porch,
wedged between two businessmen
on a flight to San Jose, cramped in the cab
of my father-in-law's truck, by the river, in a mall,
at the edges of festivals and movies,
we have settled in, Finn and I,
his cheeks fluting like small bellows,
eyes fluttering, the most ephemeral of moths.

If I practiced piano so often,
I would be good.
If my garden received such care,
it would fruit
like the arbors of Catherine the Great,
where her pensive son Pavlosk
wandered for hours.
If my breath stayed so steady,
my body so soft, and if I, and everyone else,
gave life so freely day after day,
would babies grow up
to know hunger,
anger,
war?

Leigh Hancock

What was it about the birth of my children that broke my heart open, that entered in and made itself at home? It was this wondrous love. Love I had not counted on, love I could not have anticipated, love I had not earned, love I could not prove but knew was real. Daniel followed Allen and now there are these two people in my arms, climbing on my head, throwing themselves at me, clinging to my legs. There are these people who love me, even at 6:30 a.m., crabby and sleepy and distracted as I am. They do not keep score of all my failings. They see the me I long to be when I look in the mirror, and sometimes I think all my life since they were born has been the process of becoming that woman they see, the process of a woman, in Sonia Sanchez's words, "making pilgrimage to herself." ... They imbue my life with a different kind of energy than I have known before. It is a palpable desire to make the world brand new for their sake.

Rosemary Bray McNatt, Birthing a New World

PRAYER FOR WOMEN WHO STRUGGLE TO FEED AND HOUSE THEIR FAMILIES

God of all, we believe that your sufficiency is for everyone. We know also that you require that we feed the hungry and clothe the naked from the bounty you have provided to us all.

But we also acknowledge that there are so many — especially women — who, in these times of an over-abundance of low wage jobs, struggle to keep food on their tables and roofs over their heads. And we especially remember women caught in the tattered and torn remnants of the social safety nets that have aided them in the past to feed and house themselves and their families.

We lift up for your special care those women and their children who wander among us hungry and homeless. May their sojourn lead them to caring people who will nurture them into dignity and link them with others who will share their resources with them.

Gracious God, keep nudging us toward these, the least among us. Open our hearts to hear their cries for relief and grant that we may be more faithful members of your household.

Amen.

Rev. Linda Morgan Clark

It is feminine spiritual energy, mother love, which can heal [great suffering]. A spiritually conscious mother sees behind the masks of differences into the heart of sameness. She can provide the nourishment this troubled world so sorely needs. Her heart has been stretched open to the pain and joy of loving to the point where all beings become her children. By her shining example, she brings peace to her community, the hospitals, the courtrooms, the stage, the classrooms, the Senate, and the marketplace. The world is hungry for her milk.

Jacqueline Kramer, Buddha Mom

~

AND HELP HIM COMFORT

God has
a special interest in women
for they can lift this world to their breast
and help Him
comfort.

Mirabai, sixteenth-century Hindu mystical poetess

*"How we spend our days is, of course,
how we spend our lives," mused Annie Dillard.* *

Serving breakfast
    and packing lunches;
Fastening snaps
    and tying shoes;
Doling out bandages
    and swift healing kisses;
Interrupting arguments
    and teaching how to share;
Wading through waist-high fields
    and having bouquets of dandelions
        pressed into my outstretched hands.

This is the substance of my days
    and sometimes I wonder,
Is this all there is?
    Surely I could do more.
But what work is more meaningful than this?

To feed the hungry,
    clothe the naked.
Heal the injured
    and comfort those in distress.
To teach peace and walk in this world
    with open hands,

**Annie Dillard,* The Writing Life

receiving everything —
    no matter how ordinary —
    as a treasured gift.

So let me attend to each task
    with attention and compassion,
As if the redemption of the whole world
    depended on it.

Rev. Gina Hilton-VanOsdall

~

Lord, make me an instrument of your peace.
Where there is hatred, let me sow love,
Where there is injury, pardon,
Where there is doubt, faith,
Where there is despair, hope,
Where there is darkness, light,
Where there is sadness, joy.

O Divine Master, grant that I may not so much seek
to be consoled as to console,
to be understood as to understand,
to be loved as to love.

Saint Francis of Assisi

Our love for our children brings us joy, bliss and happiness. What's really inspiring though, is that through loving a child, we deepen our capacity to be a loving person for others, too. The potential to take what we learn from loving our child and apply it to other relationships is limitless. Many mothers discover this for themselves: they feel more compassion towards other human begins, realizing they all started as precious babies worthy of a mother's devotion. These mothers discover a new potential to be patient with the surly cashier, the aggressive driver or the needy relation.

Sarah Napthali, Buddhism for Mothers

~

The mother's yearning ... feels the presence of the cherished child even in the debased, degraded man.

George Eliot, Adam Bede

Let one cultivate goodwill toward all the
world, a mind illimitable, unobstructed,
without hatred, without enmity. This mode
of loving is the supreme good.

Buddhist saying

~

Assist all "spiritual mothers," those who, though they
may have no children of their own, nevertheless selflessly care for the children of others — of every age and
state in life. Grant that they may know the joy of ful-
filling this motherly calling of women, whether in
teaching, nursing, religious life, or in other work
which recognizes and fosters the true dignity of every
human being created in Your image and likeness.

From "A Prayer for Mothers," author unknown

Without my mother I could never have known how to love. Thanks to her I can love my neighbors. Thanks to her I can love all living beings. Through her I acquired my first notions of understanding and compassion. Mother is the foundation of all love, and many religious traditions recognize this and pay deep honor to a maternal figure.

Thich Nhat Hanh, A Rose for Your Pocket

~

I'm lucky to have a faithful mother who stood with me on days when she could hardly stand for herself ... it's what I'll treasure about her all my life. Because of her example, I work hard to be a faithful mother, and I hope it's what my children eventually think of when they think of me. I hope, too, that they learn to see my faithfulness not only in my life with them, but also in my life in the world outside our home, where the need for faithfulness takes a different shape but is just as great ... they were the reasons I wanted to change the world.

Rosemary Bray McNatt, Birthing a New World

How many thousands of heroines there must be now, of whom we shall never know. But still they are there. They sow in secret the seed of which we pluck the flower, and eat the fruit, and know not that we pass the sower daily in the streets.

One form of heroism—the most common, and yet the least remembered of all—namely, the heroism of the average mother. Ah! When I think of that broad fact, I gather hope again for poor humanity; and this dark world looks bright—this diseased world looks wholesome to me once more—because, whatever else it is not full of, it is at least full of mothers.

Charles Kingsley

~

May the God who dances in creation,
and embraces us with human love,
who shakes our lives like thunder,
bless us and drive us out with power
to fill the world with her justice. Amen.

Janet Morley

Woman by nature is opposed to war; she is an advocate of peace.... Children are educated by the women.
The mother bears the troubles and anxieties of rearing
the child, undergoes the ordeal of its birth and train-
ing. Therefore, it is most difficult for mothers to send
to the battlefield those upon whom they have lavished
such love and care. Consider a son reared and trained
twenty years by a devoted mother. What sleepless
nights and restless, anxious days she has spent!
Having brought him through dangers and difficulties
to the age of maturity, how agonizing then to sacrifice
him upon the battlefield!

Therefore, the mothers will not sanction war nor
be satisfied with it. So it will come to pass that when
women participate fully and equally in the affairs of
the world ... war will cease; for woman will be the
obstacle and hindrance to it.

'Abdu'l-Bahá, Bahá'í leader

~

God could not be everywhere, and so He made mothers.

Jewish proverb

When God wants an important thing done in this world or a wrong righted, He goes about it in a very singular way. He doesn't release thunderbolts or stir up earthquakes. God simply has a tiny baby born, perhaps of a very humble home, perhaps of a very humble mother. And God puts the idea or purpose into the mother's heart. And she puts it in the baby's mind, and then — God waits.

The great events of this world are not battles and elections and earthquakes and thunderbolts. The great events are babies, for each child comes with the message that God is not yet discouraged with humanity but is still expecting good-will to become incarnate in each human life.

Attributed to Edmond McDonald

God stir the soil,
Run the ploughshare deep,
Cut the furrows round and round,
Overturn the hard, dry ground,
Spare no strength nor toil,
Even though I weep.
In the loose, fresh mangled earth
Sow new seed.
Free of withered vine and weed
Bring fair flowers to birth.

Prayer from Singapore

∼

Sow the living part of yourselves in the furrow of life.

Miguel de Unamuno

∼

As a mother at the risk of her life watches over her own child, her only child, so also let every one cultivate a boundless (friendly) mind towards all beings.

The Sutta-Nipâta, Book 1, Ch. 8:148

In the Talmud there is a story of an elderly man who was planting a carob tree beside the road. As the king traveled by, he asked the man how many years it would take before the tree would bear fruit. The man answered, "Seventy years." The king asked him if he was sure he would live long enough to see the fruit of his labors. The man replied:

"I found carob-trees in existence when I came into the world, consequently my ancestors must have planted them. Why should I not also plant them for my children?"

Babylonian Talmud, Taanit 23a

Lord, in union with your love, unite my work with your great work, and perfect it. As a drop of water, poured into a river, is taken up into the activity of the river, so may my labor become part of your work. Thus may those among whom I live and work be drawn into your love.

Saint Gertrude the Great

When the Ethiopian mother died in childbirth, her baby was almost buried alive with her. Just as they tossed gravel and dirt into the grave, a woman grabbed the child and ran to Pokwo, the Village of Life, where she gave the infant to a mother whose five babies died at birth.

account from The Spokesman Review

~

VILLAGE OF LIFE

For the women and children of Gambella, Ethiopia

Did she hear the cries
before she saw the shape
in the distance—woman running,
baby on her back, a ghost of dust
haunting the road behind her?

Did she take the child then in her own arms,
as her own child home from the grave, and learn
how it felt to hold a baby that lived?
Brushing flies that swarmed
the child's mouth like a sweet, red fruit.

Did she wrap the child against her chest,
and carry her to the river's edge? The baby
kicking at her hollow belly,

rooting at the leather
of her cracked breasts.

Did she hold her in the cool river,
try to wash away the dust, black dirt,
the memory of clinging to her mother
     in the earth?
The air heavy with the smell of dung and vultures
circling the herd of burned-out cattle bones.

Did she join the baby in the current
of the Baro River, floating on the water
as in birth? The voice of the river drowning
the wail of her own keen. Rising
in its place, their lullaby—

From birth to grave to water's edge,
from buried love
to life.

Lynn L. Caruso

Note: All across Africa, women are taking on the responsibility of raising children who have lost their parents to AIDS, genocide, and the repercussions of poverty. Tragically, in the amount of time it took you to read this page, six children were orphaned worldwide by AIDS alone (statistic provided by World Vision). See "Editor's Note," pages 242–43.

THE SUN NEVER SAYS

Even
after
all this time
the sun never says to the earth,

"You owe me."

Look
what happens
with a love like that—

it lights the whole
world.

Hafiz, fourteenth-century Persian mystic

A BENEDICTION

We know what God requires of us:
to do justice,
to love kindness,
and to walk humbly with our God.

Now may the God of all mother love,
the God of all healing,
and the Spirit of all compassion,
meet you,
and bless you,
and send you forth.

Go in God's Peace.
Rev. Lauren J. McFeaters

About the Contributors

Angelou, Maya, American poet, historian, educator, civil rights activist, and author of twelve best-selling books.

Arjan, Dev (1563–1606), poet and the fifth Guru of Sikhism, martyred in 1606.

Babel, Isaac (1894–1940), Soviet author, journalist, and playwright. He was arrested in 1939 on charges of espionage; it's believed he was executed shortly thereafter.

'Abdu'l-Bahá, (1844–1921), leader of the Bahá'í faith and prolific writer.

Bain, Sarah K., mother to Grace, who soars, and three more who remain grounded; has stories, poems, and essays in numerous publications. Facilitator for the MISS Foundation.

Baker, Winona L., Canadian poet, mother of four children; best known for Japanese forms of haiku and tanka, she is the author of six published books of poetry.

Bass, Ellen, writing teacher in the MFA program at Pacific University; author of several nonfiction books and four books of poetry, including *The Human Line*, 2007.

Beil, Rev. Susie Crawford, mother of three and pastor for Children and Families at Opportunity Presbyterian Church in Spokane, Washington.

Big Thunder, late nineteenth-century member of the Algonquin nation.

Black, Kathryn, lecturer and author of *Mothering without a Map*, 2004.

Bodenstab, Johanna, translator, freelance journalist, and writer. Graduate of the Psychoanalysis for Scholars program at Western New England Institute for Psychoanalysis.

Brontë, Emily (1818–1848), British poet and author of the classic, *Wuthering Heights*; also published under Ellis Bell.

Buber, Martin (1878–1965), Jewish philosopher born in Vienna and author of *I and Thou*.

Campos-Davis, DeLona, writer, teacher, and doula. DeLona resides in Hood River, Oregon, where she learns the daily lessons of motherhood from her three boys.

Carlyle, Jane Welsh (1801–1866), notable Scottish letter writer and wife of essayist Thomas Carlyle.

Chesterton, Gilbert Keith (1874–1936), English writer, poet, and essayist; best known for his popular detective stories of Father Brown.

Clark, Rev. Linda Morgan, United Methodist Church clergy; former executive director of the Oklahoma Religious Coalition for Reproductive Choice, 1993–2005.

DeGrandis, Fr. Robert, Catholic priest who has written more than forty books, including *The Ten Commandments of Prayer*.

Diamant, Anita, Jewish author, whose many publications include the bestseller *The Red Tent*, 1997.

Douthitt, Mary, writer living in Spokane, Washington. Her work has appeared in national and regional publications.

Eliot, George (1819–1880), English novelist and a leading writer of the Victorian era; best known for her novel *Middlemarch*.

Ephrem, Saint (c. 306–373), Greek poet, hymn writer, and theologian; more than 400 of his hymns remain today.

Euripides (480–406 BCE), Greek poet and playwright of more than ninety-two plays.

Finley, Kathleen, teacher, speaker, and writer on issues of spirituality; mother of three whose recent publications include *The Liturgy of Motherhood*.

Francis of Assisi, Saint (c. 1181–1226), Christian saint who founded the Franciscan religious order and is known for his love of all creatures.

Fromm, Erich (1900–1980), German-born psychoanalyst, best known for his work *Escape from Freedom*, 1941.

Frost, Robert (1874–1963), American poet and teacher whose prolific body of plays and poetry gained him four Pulitzer prizes.

Gertrude the Great, Saint (1256–1302), Benedictine and mystic writer; well known for her *Herald of Divine Love*.

Gibran, Kahlil (1883–1931), Lebanese-American poet, artist, and author of numerous books, including his best known, *The Prophet*.

Gillan, Maria Mazziotti, cultural activist, editor, and author of eight books of poetry; professor and director of the Creative Writing Program at Binghamton University.

Goldblatt, Stacey, poet and author of the novel *Stray*, 2007.

Grace of Monaco, Princess (1929–1982), Academy-award-winning American actress who married Rainier III of Monaco in 1956 to become the Princess of Monaco.

Hafiz (1310–1341), Persian Sufi poet who wrote nearly five thousand poems, primarily addressing the spiritual experience of a mystic.

Hancock, Leigh, Northwestern poet and writer who is learning to see the demands of parenting and family life as inspiration rather than obstacle to the writing life.

Hanh, Thich Nhat, Vietnamese Buddhist monk and prolific writer whose teaching of "mindfulness meditation" has influenced the world.

Hays, Fr. Edward, teacher, author of eighteen books, and founder of the Shantivanam house of prayer.

Hebblethwaite, Margaret, British Catholic journalist, editor, and feminist author of numerous books; founder of the Santa Maria Education Fund in Paraguay.

Heil, Jackie, foster mother from Kansas who has cared for more than one hundred babies waiting to be adopted.

Hershey, Sibilla, clinical social worker and writer; born in Riga, Latvia; came to the United States at age sixteen as a World War II displaced person; currently lives in Davis, CA.

Hewitt, Lauri, glass artist living with her family near Puget Sound on the Kitsap Peninsula.

Hilton-VanOsdall, Rev. Gina, ordained minister in the Presbyterian Church (USA); served ten years as a pastor and then "retired" to raise and enjoy her three young children.

Hokanson, Alicia, poet and teacher from Seattle, Washington. Her three collections of poetry are *Phosphorous*, *Mapping the Distance*, and *Insistent in the Skin*.

Hopkins, Gerard Manley (1844–1889), English Jesuit priest whose lyrical, spiritual poetry reflected his view of poetry as an "inner landscape."

Hopkins, Jill E, mother, psychotherapist, and author of *Welcoming the Soul of a Child*, 1999.

Huffman, Margaret Anne (1941–2000), American writer whose numerous publications include *A Moment with God for Mothers*.

Hunt, Linda Lawrence, director of the Krista Foundation for Global Citizenship; author of *Bold Spirit*; former English professor at Whitworth University.

Hurdle, Crystal, guest poet at the University of Oxford, October 2007, and author of *After Ted & Sylvia: Poems*; teaches creative writing and English at Capilano College, British Columbia.

Jensen, Jane Richardson, American translator and author of *She Who Prays: A Woman's Interfaith Prayer Book*; chaplain of Clare's Place, a women's spirituality center in Texas.

John of the Cross, Saint (1542–1591), Christian mystical philosopher and writer.

Julian of Norwich (1342–1416), English mystic whose divine vision was recorded in her book *Sixteen Revelations of Divine Love*; her writings explore maternal qualities of God.

Kabir (1440–1518), mystical Hindu poet in India who was influenced by the mystic Sufi branch of Islam.

Khan, Hazrat Inayat, Sufi master, first brought Sufism to the Western world; his writings include sixteen volumes of collected works.

Kingsley, Charles (1819–1875), English author and clergyman who served as chaplain to Queen Victoria.

Klein, Laurie, award-winning writer whose works are widely published. Co-founder of *Rock & Sling*, she also wrote the now-classic chorus "I Love You, Lord."

Kramer, Jacqueline, spiritual counselor, teacher, and author of *Buddha Mom*, 2004.

Lacordaire, Jean Baptiste (1802–1861), French Catholic preacher and journalist who is viewed as a founding father of modern Catholicism.

Lam, Fiona Tinwei, Scottish-born Chinese-Canadian poet, author of *Intimate Distances*, and editor of *Double Lives: Writing and Motherhood*.

Lamott, Anne, American author of three works of nonfiction and six novels; recipient of the Guggenheim fellowship and author of the best-selling *Traveling Mercies*.

Lao-Tzu (born c. 600 BCE), Chinese philosopher known for his treatise, *Tao Te Ching*, a basis for the Taoist religion and very influential in Zen Buddhism.

Lawrence, D. H. (1885–1930), English novelist, poet, short-story writer, and essayist who profoundly influenced modern English fiction.

Liebert, Dr. Donald, retired professor of sociology, Whitworth University; visiting professor, Forman Christian College, Lahore, Pakistan; advocate for issues of social justice and beloved grandfather of eight.

McFeaters, Rev. Lauren J., associate pastor at Nassau Presbyterian Church in Princeton, New Jersey. A published preacher and liturgist, pastoral counselor, and mother of five-year-old Josie.

McKeating, Rev. Dr. Henry (1932–2005), writer and senior lecturer in theology at the University of Nottingham.

McLaughlin, Lauren, co-minister, with her husband, John, of UnityNow, a Spiritual Learning Center on the Internet at www.unitynow.com.

McNatt, Rosemary Bray, Unitarian Universalist minister and former editor of the *New York Times Book Review*; author of several books.

Meehan, Maude, author of three books of poetry and a collection of poems spanning twenty years, *Washing the Stones*; has taught workshops at University of California, Santa Cruz, and is widely anthologized.

Minato, Amy Klauke, teacher and poet whose publications include the collection of poems *The Wider Lens*.

Mirabai (c. 1498–1550), the most celebrated female poet-saint of India. Born a princess, yet spent many years caring for the destitute.

Mistral, Gabriela (1889–1957), pseudonym for Lucila Godoy y Alcayaga, Chilean poet, educator, and feminist. First Latin American to win the Nobel Prize in Literature, 1945.

Morley, Janet, British writer and former director of Christian Aid in the United Kingdom; author of *All Desires Known*.

Murphy, Claire Rudolf, a writer whose numerous books for young readers have been inspired by her grown children Conor and Megan, and her mother Frances. She is coauthor of *Daughters of the Desert: Stories of Remarkable Women from Christian, Jewish, and Muslim Traditions* (Woodstock, VT: SkyLight Paths Publishing) www.clairerudolfmurphy.com.

Napthali, Sarah, Australian writer and author of *Buddhism for Mothers: A Calm Approach to Caring for Yourself and Your Children*.

Nivedita, Sister (Margaret E. Noble) (1867–1911), Irish author, social worker, and follower of Swami Vivekananda; moved to India in 1895 to serve the disenfranchised.

Norris, Gunilla, psychotherapist and author of eleven children's books, five books exploring spirituality in the everyday, and one book of poems.

Parker, Theodore (1810–1860), Unitarian minister, theologian, and social reformer.

Paulus, Christine Ryan, birth mother with immeasurable gratitude to her daughter and her parents. A hairdresser who has published poetry and a computer book. Her most precious gift was meeting and continuing a relationship with her daughter.

Payne, Margaret G., author and bishop of the New England synod of the Evangelical Lutheran Church in America.

Penn, William (1644–1718), pacifist Quaker who founded Pennsylvania and implemented a democratic system of governance.

Petronius (c. 27–66), Roman writer and author of *The Satyricon*.

Po Chü-i (772–846), prolific Chinese poet of the T'ang dynasty.

Reynolds, Jan, award-winning photographer, adventurist, and author of *The Vanishing Culture* series for children.

Rivage (pseudonym for Mary Newman), poet and visual artist who strongly believes in the power of that shared Spirit with which each natural entity is imbued.

Robinson, William H. (1848–1923), born a slave in North Carolina; Civil War veteran, minister, and author of *Fifteen Years in Slavery*.

Rossetti, Christina (1830–1894), British poet closely connected to the Pre-Raphaelite Brotherhood (a group of religious painters).

Russell, George William (1867–1935), Irish author who wrote under pseudonym of AE. Major influence in the Irish literary renaissance.

Sappho (630 BC–570 BC), ancient Greek poet whose poems have been immortalized through the writings of others; only a single poem by her has survived in complete form.

Sasso, Rabbi Sandy Eisenberg, author of many award-winning children's books including *God's Paintbrush* and *In God's Name* (Woodstock, VT: Jewish Lights Publishing).

Sayres, Meghan Nuttall, is a tapestry weaver and author of *Anahita's Woven Riddle*, a novel set in Iran; *Weaving Tapestry in Rural Ireland*; and coauthor of *Daughters of the Desert: Stories of Remarkable Women from Christian, Jewish, and Muslim Traditions* (Woodstock, VT: SkyLight Paths Publishing).

Schwartz, Edythe Haendel, retired faculty, Department of Child Development, CSU Sacramento; widely published poet in anthologies and journals such as *Calyx* and *JAMA*.

Sen, Ramprasad (1718–1775), Indian poet saint whose works include *Grace and Mercy in Her Wild Hair: Selected Poems to the Mother Goddess*.

Shakespeare, William (1564–1616), English poet and playwright of more than thirty plays.

Shields, Trish, her poetry and short stories have been published internationally. Her works include the book of poetry *Soul Speak*, and her coauthored chapbook, *Coast Lines*.

Shiki, Masaoka (1867–1902), Japanese poet who infused traditional haiku with a new naturalistic aesthetic.

Singh, Sadhu Sundar (1889–1929), Indian Christian missionary, raised as a Sikh but converted to Christianity after his mother's death.

Starr, Mirabai, writer, teacher, speaker, and acclaimed translator of numerous books, including the recent *Teresa of Avila: The Book of My Life*.

Steer, Janeen, mother of three young children, attended Princeton Theological Seminary where she earned a Master of Divinity and a Master of Education.

Swift, Jonathan (1667–1745), Irish cleric, journalist, author, and renowned satirist best known for *Gulliver's Travels*.

Tagore, Rabindranath (1861–1941), Indian poet, philosopher, and social reformer who won the Nobel Prize in literature.

Thoreau, Henry David (1817–1862), American author best known for his book *Walden* and for his embrace of nature and transcendentalism.

Tukaram (1608–1649), Indian mystic who composed more than five thousand mystical songs.

Twain, Mark (1835–1910), pseudonym of Samuel Clemens, American writer and humorist; best known for *The Adventures of Huckleberry Finn*.

Unamuno, Miguel de (1864–1963), Spanish novelist, poet, and playwright.

Vivekananda, Swami (1863–1902), renowned spiritual leader of Vedanta and Yoga philosophies whose writings fill nine volumes.

Waggoner, Gloria, artist, writer, and organic/environmental living methods instructor. Creator and Curator of the fair trade boutique, Rosa Gallica LifeStyle.

Waldenberg, Sophia, eight-year-old student from Spokane, Washington. Her hobbies include snow skiing, soccer, and ballet.

Walker, Jeanne Murray, award-winning poet whose seven volumes include *Coming into History*, 1991, and *A Deed to the Light*, 2004.

Webber, Robert E. (1933–2007), theologian and author of more than forty books.

Woodroffe, John (1865–1936), author who wrote under pseudonym Arthur Avalon. His books, including *The Serpent Power*, fostered widespread interest in Hinduism.

Woolf, Virginia (1882–1941), English author, feminist, and critic who is best remembered for her classic feminist work, *A Room of One's Own*.

Credits

Many thanks to the editors of the following magazines in which this material first appeared, and to the authors who generously granted permission to reprint.

Mothering, "Communion" by Lynn Caruso; "A Moment of Grace" by Mary Douthitt is an excerpt of the essay "Losing Isabel," originally published in *Parents Magazine*, November 2003; *Mothering*, "A Mother's Nature" by Stacey Goldblatt; *Mothering*, "Nursing Finn" by Leigh Hancock; *Arches* (Autumn 2000), "A Terrible Beauty" by Linda Lawrence Hunt; *Room of One's Own*, "Births and Deaths" by Crystal Hurdle; *Radix Magazine* (32:2), "St. Kevin's Blackbird" by Laurie Klein; *Contemporary Verse II*, "Park" by Fiona Tinwei Lam; *Mothering*, "In Flight" by Amy Klauke Minato; *JAMA*, (January 17, 2007); "Habañera" by Edythe Haendel Schwartz; *Poetry*, "The Shawl," "Birth," and "Seizure" by Jeanne Murray Walker

※ ※ ※

Two haiku by Winona Baker. Reprinted with permission of Winona Baker, © 2007.

"There Are Times in Life When One Does the Right Thing," by Ellen Bass, originally published in *Our Stunning Harvest* by Autumn Press. Used by permission of Ellen Bass.

Ellen Bass, "For My Daughter on Her Twenty-first Birthday" from *Mules of Love*. Copyright © 2002 by Ellen Bass. Reprinted with the permission of BOA Editions, Ltd., www.boaeditions.org.

Excerpt from the sermon "The God Who Feeds," by Susie Crawford Beil. Reprinted with permission of Susie Crawford Beil, © 2007.

"The Beginning," from *Mothering without a Map* by Kathryn Black, copyright © 2004 by Kathryn Black. Used by permission of Viking Penguin, a division of Penguin Group (USA) Inc.

"Under Siege: A Mother-Daughter Relationship Survives the Holocaust" by Johanna Bodenstab. Reprinted with permission from *Psychoanalytic Inquiry*, 24 (5), 2004, Analytic Press, Taylor & Francis Group, www.informaworld.com. Video testimony is from the Holocaust Video Testimony (#34) housed at the Fortunoff Video Archive for Holocaust Testimonies, Yale University.

"Bless This Belly," "Tonglen for Mothers," and "I Find Traces of You in My Mothering," by DeLona Campos-Davis. Reprinted with permission of DeLona Campos-Davis, © 2007.

"Prayer for Women Who Struggle to Feed and House Their Families," by Rev. Linda Morgan Clark. Used by permission of the Religious Coalition for Reproductive Choice, www.rcrc.org.

"Pledge for an Adopted Child," as reprinted in *Celebrating Your New Jewish Daughter: Creating Jewish Ways to Welcome Baby Girls into the Covenant—New and Traditional Ceremonies* (c) 2001 Debra Nussbaum Cohen (Woodstock, VT: Jewish Lights Publishing). Permission granted by Jewish Lights Publishing, P.O. Box 237, Woodstock, VT 05091, www.jewishlights.com.

Two prayers from *The Ten Commandments of Prayer* by Fr. Robert DeGrandis, S.S.J. Contact at DeGrandis/Kittley, www.degran disssj.com, 17 Oak Harbor Drive, Houston, Texas 77062 U.S.A.

Acknowledgments

Special thanks to my parents, Don and Doris Liebert; Mary Caruso; Janeen Steer; Deb Gore; my writing group: Meghan Nuttall Sayres, Mary Cronk Farrell, Mary Douthitt, Claire Rudolf Murphy; and my editors Emily Wichland, Jessica Swift, and Marcia Broucek, for their insight and expertise. To all of the friends who have influenced who I am as a mother and find themselves in the pages of this collection. To Patrick, whose devotion to our family is another book altogether. And finally to our three sons, Isaac, Samuel, and Eli, for being the life behind these words.

Editor's Note

Throughout *Honoring Motherhood*, I have referenced a number of organizations that work directly on issues of justice for women and children around the world. Below you will find further descriptions and contact information for these organizations. This is just a starting place. I hope that this collection has served to nourish and replenish you as a mother and that, in turn, you will sow seeds of love out into the greater world.

The Krista Foundation

In the spring of 1998, my close friend, Linda Lawrence Hunt, tragically lost her daughter in a bus accident in Bolivia. In time, she channeled her profound grief and enduring love into creating a foundation that supports young people engaged in service work throughout the world. To learn more about the foundation, named in honor of her daughter, visit the Krista Foundation Web site at www.kristafoundation.org.

The Anuak of Gambella, Ethiopia

The orphaned baby, in the poem on page 222, is now an adult woman, named Ariet Oman, living in the United States. On December 13, 2003, Ariet learned that over 400 men and boys of her Anuak tribe were massacred in Gambella, Ethiopia. Since that time she has helped to establish the Anuak Meer (love) Ministry to provide assistance to widows and orphans who are victims of genocide, AIDS, and poverty in Ethiopia. Tragically, the genocide continues. To read more about the Anuak Meer Ministry, visit www.spokanefpc.org/Mission/AnuakMeer Ministry/tabid/1594/Default.aspx. For further information on the Anuak people, visit the Anuak Justice Council's Web site at www.anuakjustice.org.

Grupo de Apoyo Mutuo (GAM) "Group of Mutual Support"

In June of 1984, twenty-five wives and mothers of "disappeared" Guatemalans came together to form this group. Originally, they focused their efforts on searching for their own family members, but their suffering has since united them in a common cause. Tragically, through decades of civil unrest, more than 90,000 individuals have "disappeared" in Latin America, and through the use of nonviolent action, GAM continues to be a strong voice for human rights in Guatemala.

My Own Special Prayers, Blessings & Memories

My Own Special Prayers, Blessings & Memories

My Own Special Prayers, Blessings & Memories

My Own Special Prayers, Blessings & Memories

My Own Special Prayers, Blessings & Memories

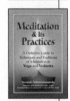

Judaism / Christianity / Interfaith

Talking about God: Exploring the Meaning of Religious Life with Kierkegaard, Buber, Tillich and Heschel *by Daniel F. Polish, PhD*
Examines the meaning of the human religious experience with the greatest theologians of modern times. 6 x 9, 176 pp, HC, 978-1-59473-230-0 **$21.99**

Interactive Faith: The Essential Interreligious Community-Building Handbook
Edited by Rev. Bud Heckman with Rori Picker Neiss
A guide to the key methods and resources of the interfaith movement.
6 x 9, 400 pp (est), HC, 978-1-59473-237-9 **$40.00**

The Jewish Approach to Repairing the World (*Tikkun Olam*)
A Brief Introduction for Christians *by Rabbi Elliot N. Dorff, PhD*
A window into the Jewish idea of responsibility to care for the world.
5½ x 8½, 192 pp (est), Quality PB, 978-1-58023-349-1 **$16.99** (a Jewish Lights book)

Modern Jews Engage the New Testament: Enhancing Jewish Well-Being in a Christian Environment *by Rabbi Michael J. Cook, PhD*
A look at the dynamics of the New Testament.
6 x 9, 400 pp (est), HC, 978-1-58023-313-2 **$29.99** (a Jewish Lights book)

Disaster Spiritual Care: Practical Clergy Responses to Community, Regional and National Tragedy
Edited by Rabbi Stephen B. Roberts, BCJC, & Rev. Willard W.C. Ashley, Sr., DMin, DH
The definitive reference for pastoral caregivers of all faiths involved in disaster response.
6 x 9, 384 pp, Hardcover, 978-1-59473-240-9 **$40.00**

The Changing Christian World: A Brief Introduction for Jews
by Rabbi Leonard A. Schoolman
5½ x 8½, 176 pp, Quality PB, 978-1-58023-344-6 **$16.99** (a Jewish Lights book)

The Jewish Connection to Israel, the Promised Land: A Brief Introduction for Christians *by Rabbi Eugene Korn, PhD*
5½ x 8½, 192 pp, Quality PB, 978-1-58023-318-7 **$14.99** (a Jewish Lights book)

Christians and Jews in Dialogue: Learning in the Presence of the Other
by Mary C. Boys and Sara S. Lee; Foreword by Dorothy C. Bass
Inspires renewed commitment to dialogue between religious traditions.
6 x 9, 240 pp, HC, 978-1-59473-144-0 **$21.99**

Healing the Jewish-Christian Rift: Growing Beyond Our Wounded History
by Ron Miller and Laura Bernstein; Foreword by Dr. Beatrice Bruteau
6 x 9, 288 pp, Quality PB, 978-1-59473-139-6 **$18.99**

Introducing My Faith and My Community
The Jewish Outreach Institute Guide for the Christian in a Jewish Interfaith Relationship
by Rabbi Kerry M. Olitzky 6 x 9, 176 pp, Quality PB, 978-1-58023-192-3 **$16.99** *(a Jewish Lights book)*

The Jewish Approach to God: A Brief Introduction for Christians
by Rabbi Neil Gillman 5½ x 8½, 192 pp, Quality PB, 978-1-58023-190-9 **$16.95** *(a Jewish Lights book)*

Jewish Holidays: A Brief Introduction for Christians
by Rabbi Kerry M. Olitzky and Rabbi Daniel Judson
5½ x 8½, 176 pp, Quality PB, 978-1-58023-302-6 **$16.99** *(a Jewish Lights book)*

Jewish Ritual: A Brief Introduction for Christians
by Rabbi Kerry M. Olitzky and Rabbi Daniel Judson
5½ x 8½, 144 pp, Quality PB, 978-1-58023-210-4 **$14.99** *(a Jewish Lights book)*

Jewish Spirituality: A Brief Introduction for Christians *by Rabbi Lawrence Kushner*
5½ x 8½, 112 pp, Quality PB, 978-1-58023-150-3 **$12.95** *(a Jewish Lights book)*

A Jewish Understanding of the New Testament
by Rabbi Samuel Sandmel; new Preface by Rabbi David Sandmel
5½ x 8½, 368 pp, Quality PB, 978-1-59473-048-1 **$19.99**

We Jews and Jesus: Exploring Theological Differences for Mutual Understanding
by Rabbi Samuel Sandmel; new Preface by Rabbi David Sandmel A Classic Reprint
6 x 9, 192 pp, Quality PB, 978-1-59473-208-9 **$16.99**

Show Me Your Way: The Complete Guide to Exploring Interfaith Spiritual Direction
by Howard A. Addison 5½ x 8½, 240 pp, Quality PB, 978-1-893361-41-6 **$16.95**

Spiritual Poetry—The Mystic Poets

Experience these mystic poets as you never have before. Each beautiful, compact book includes: a brief introduction to the poet's time and place; a summary of the major themes of the poet's mysticism and religious tradition; essential selections from the poet's most important works; and an appreciative preface by a contemporary spiritual writer.

Hafiz
The Mystic Poets
Preface by Ibrahim Gamard
Hafiz is known throughout the world as Persia's greatest poet, with sales of his poems in Iran today only surpassed by those of the Qur'an itself. His probing and joyful verse speaks to people from all backgrounds who long to taste and feel divine love and experience harmony with all living things.
5 x 7¼, 144 pp, HC, 978-1-59473-009-2 **$16.99**

Hopkins
The Mystic Poets
Preface by Rev. Thomas Ryan, CSP
Gerard Manley Hopkins, Christian mystical poet, is beloved for his use of fresh language and startling metaphors to describe the world around him. Although his verse is lovely, beneath the surface lies a searching soul, wrestling with and yearning for God.
5 x 7¼, 112 pp, HC, 978-1-59473-010-8 **$16.99**

Tagore
The Mystic Poets
Preface by Swami Adiswarananda
Rabindranath Tagore is often considered the "Shakespeare" of modern India. A great mystic, Tagore was the teacher of W. B. Yeats and Robert Frost, the close friend of Albert Einstein and Mahatma Gandhi, and the winner of the Nobel Prize for Literature. This beautiful sampling of Tagore's two most important works, *The Gardener* and *Gitanjali*, offers a glimpse into his spiritual vision that has inspired people around the world.
5 x 7¼, 144 pp, HC, 978-1-59473-008-5 **$16.99**

Whitman
The Mystic Poets
Preface by Gary David Comstock
Walt Whitman was the most innovative and influential poet of the nineteenth century. This beautiful sampling of Whitman's most important poetry from *Leaves of Grass*, and selections from his prose writings, offers a glimpse into the spiritual side of his most radical themes—love for country, love for others, and love of Self.
5 x 7¼, 192 pp, HC, 978-1-59473-041-2 **$16.99**

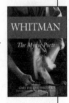

Journeys of Simplicity
Traveling Light with Thomas Merton, Bashō,
Edward Abbey, Annie Dillard & Others
Invites you to consider a more graceful way of traveling through life.
Use the included journal pages (in PB only) to help you get started on
your own spiritual journey.

Ed. by Philip Harnden
5 x 7¼, 144 pp, Quality PB, 978-1-59473-181-5 **$12.99**
128 pp, HC, 978-1-893361-76-8 **$16.95**

Children's Spirituality

Adam and Eve's First Sunset: God's New Day
by Sandy Eisenberg Sasso; Full-color illus. by Joani Keller Rothenberg
9 x 12, 32 pp, Full-color illus., HC, 978-1-58023-177-0 **$17.95** *For ages 4 & up (a Jewish Lights book)*

Because Nothing Looks Like God
by Lawrence and Karen Kushner; Full-color illus. by Dawn W. Majewski
Real-life examples of happiness and sadness introduce children to the possibilities of spiritual life. 11 x 8½, 32 pp, HC, Full-color illus., 978-1-58023-092-6 **$16.95**
For ages 4 & up (a Jewish Lights book)

Also available: **Teacher's Guide,** 8½ x 11, 22 pp, PB, 978-1-58023-140-4 **$6.95** *For ages 5–8*

Becoming Me: A Story of Creation
by Martin Boroson; Full-color illus. by Christopher Gilvan-Cartwright
Told in the personal "voice" of the Creator, a story about creation and relationship that is about each one of us.
8 x 10, 32 pp, Full-color illus., HC, 978-1-893361-11-9 **$16.95** *For ages 4 & up*

But God Remembered: Stories of Women from Creation to the
Promised Land *by Sandy Eisenberg Sasso; Full-color illus. by Bethanne Andersen*
A fascinating collection of four different stories of women only briefly mentioned in biblical tradition and religious texts. 9 x 12, 32 pp, HC, Full-color illus., 978-1-879045-43-9 **$16.95**
For ages 8 & up (a Jewish Lights book)

Cain & Abel: Finding the Fruits of Peace
by Sandy Eisenberg Sasso; Full-color illus. by Joani Keller Rothenberg
A sensitive recasting of the ancient tale shows we have the power to deal with anger in positive ways. "Editor's Choice"—American Library Association's *Booklist*
9 x 12, 32 pp, HC, Full-color illus., 978-1-58023-123-7 **$16.95** *For ages 5 & up (a Jewish Lights book)*

Does God Hear My Prayer?
by August Gold; Full-color photos by Diane Hardy Waller
Introduces preschoolers and young readers to prayer and how it helps them express their own emotions. 10 x 8½, 32 pp, Quality PB, Full-color photo illus., 978-1-59473-102-0 **$8.99**

The 11th Commandment: Wisdom from Our Children *by The Children of America*
"If there were an Eleventh Commandment, what would it be?" Children of many religious denominations across America answer this question—in their own drawings and words. "A rare book of spiritual celebration for all people, of all ages, for all time." —*Bookviews*
8 x 10, 48 pp, HC, Full-color illus., 978-1-879045-46-0 **$16.95** *For all ages (a Jewish Lights book)*

For Heaven's Sake *by Sandy Eisenberg Sasso; Full-color illus. by Kathryn Kunz Finney*
Everyone talked about heaven: "Thank heavens." "Heaven forbid." "For heaven's sake, Isaiah." But no one would say what heaven was or how to find it. So Isaiah decides to find out, by seeking answers from many different people.
9 x 12, 32 pp, HC, Full-color illus., 978-1-58023-054-4 **$16.95** *For ages 4 & up (a Jewish Lights book)*

God in Between *by Sandy Eisenberg Sasso; Full-color illus. by Sally Sweetland*
A magical, mythical tale that teaches that God can be found where we are.
9 x 12, 32 pp, HC, Full-color illus., 978-1-879045-86-6 **$16.95** *For ages 4 & up (a Jewish Lights book)*

God's Paintbrush: Special 10th Anniversary Edition
Invites children of all faiths and backgrounds to encounter God through moments in their own lives. 11 x 8½, 32 pp, Full-color illus., HC, 978-1-58023-195-4 **$17.95** *For ages 4 & up*

Also available: **God's Paintbrush Teacher's Guide** 8½ x 11, 32 pp, 978-1-879045-57-6 **$8.95**

God's Paintbrush Celebration Kit
A Spiritual Activity Kit for Teachers and Students of All Faiths, All Backgrounds
Additional activity sheets available:
8-Student Activity Sheet Pack (40 sheets/5 sessions), 978-1-58023-058-2 **$19.95**
Single-Student Activity Sheet Pack (5 sessions), 978-1-58023-059-9 **$3.95**

Children's Spiritual Biography

Ten Amazing People
And How They Changed the World
by Maura D. Shaw; Foreword by Dr. Robert Coles
Full-color illus. by Stephen Marchesi

For ages
7 & up

Black Elk • Dorothy Day • Malcolm X • Mahatma Gandhi • Martin Luther King, Jr. • Mother Teresa • Janusz Korczak • Desmond Tutu • Thich Nhat Hanh • Albert Schweitzer

This vivid, inspirational and authoritative book will open new possibilities for children by telling the stories of how ten of the past century's greatest leaders changed the world in important ways.
8½ x 11, 48 pp, HC, Full-color illus., 978-1-893361-47-8 **$17.95**
For ages 7 & up

Spiritual Biographies for Young People—For ages 7 and up

Black Elk: Native American Man of Spirit
by Maura D. Shaw; Full-color illus. by Stephen Marchesi
Through historically accurate illustrations and photos, inspiring age-appropriate activities and Black Elk's own words, this colorful biography introduces children to a remarkable person who ensured that the traditions and beliefs of his people would not be forgotten.
6¾ x 8¾, 32 pp, HC, Full-color and b/w illus., 978-1-59473-043-6 **$12.99**

Dorothy Day: A Catholic Life of Action
by Maura D. Shaw; Full-color illus. by Stephen Marchesi
Introduces children to one of the most inspiring women of the twentieth century, a down-to-earth spiritual leader who saw the presence of God in every person she met. Includes practical activities, a timeline and a list of important words to know.
6¾ x 8¾, 32 pp, HC, Full-color illus., 978-1-59473-011-5 **$12.99**

Gandhi: India's Great Soul
by Maura D. Shaw; Full-color illus. by Stephen Marchesi
There are a number of biographies of Gandhi written for young readers, but this is the only one that balances a simple text with illustrations, photographs, and activities that encourage children and adults to talk about how to make changes happen without violence. Introduces children to important concepts of freedom, equality and justice among people of all backgrounds and religions.
6¾ x 8¾, 32 pp, HC, Full-color illus., 978-1-893361-91-1 **$12.95**

Thich Nhat Hanh: Buddhism in Action
by Maura D. Shaw; Full-color illus. by Stephen Marchesi
Warm illustrations, photos, age-appropriate activities and Thich Nhat Hanh's own poems introduce a great man to children in a way they can understand and enjoy. Includes a list of important Buddhist words to know.
6¾ x 8¾, 32 pp, HC, Full-color illus., 978-1-893361-87-4 **$12.95**

Children's Spirituality—Board Books

Adam and Eve's New Day (A Board Book)
by Sandy Eisenberg Sasso; Full-color illus. by Joani Keller Rothenberg
A lesson in hope for every child who has worried about what comes next. Abridged from *Adam and Eve's First Sunset*.
5 x 5, 24 pp, Full-color illus., Board Book, 978-1-59473-205-8 **$7.99** *For ages 0–4*

How Did the Animals Help God? (A Board Book)
by Nancy Sohn Swartz; Full-color illus. by Melanie Hall
Abridged from *In Our Image*, God asks all of nature to offer gifts to humankind—with a promise that they will care for creation in return.
5 x 5, 24 pp, Board Book, Full-color illus., 978-1-59473-044-3 **$7.99** *For ages 0–4*

Where Is God? (A Board Book) *by Lawrence and Karen Kushner; Full-color illus. by Dawn W. Majewski* A gentle way for young children to explore how God is with us every day, in every way. Abridged from *Because Nothing Looks Like God*.
5 x 5, 24 pp, Board Book, Full-color illus., 978-1-893361-17-1 **$7.99** *For ages 0–4*

What Does God Look Like? (A Board Book)
by Lawrence and Karen Kushner; Full-color illus. by Dawn W. Majewski
A simple way for young children to explore the ways that we "see" God. Abridged from *Because Nothing Looks Like God*.
5 x 5, 24 pp, Board Book, Full-color illus., 978-1-893361-23-2 **$7.99** *For ages 0–4*

How Does God Make Things Happen? (A Board Book)
by Lawrence and Karen Kushner; Full-color illus. by Dawn W. Majewski
A charming invitation for young children to explore how God makes things happen in our world. Abridged from *Because Nothing Looks Like God*.
5 x 5, 24 pp, Board Book, Full-color illus., 978-1-893361-24-9 **$7.99** *For ages 0–4*

What Is God's Name? (A Board Book)
by Sandy Eisenberg Sasso; Full-color illus. by Phoebe Stone
Everyone and everything in the world has a name. What is God's name? Abridged from the award-winning *In God's Name*.
5 x 5, 24 pp, Board Book, Full-color illus., 978-1-893361-10-2 **$7.99** *For ages 0–4*

What You Will See Inside ...

This important new series of books, each with many full-color photos, is designed to show children ages 6 and up the Who, What, When, Where, Why and How of traditional houses of worship, liturgical celebrations, and rituals of different world faiths, empowering them to respect and understand their own religious traditions—and those of their friends and neighbors.

What You Will See Inside a Catholic Church
by Reverend Michael Keane; Foreword by Robert J. Keeley, EdD
Full-color photos by Aaron Pepis
8½ x 10½, 32 pp, Full-color photos, HC, 978-1-893361-54-6 **$17.95**

Also available in Spanish: **Lo que se puede ver dentro de una iglesia católica**
8½ x 10½, 32 pp, Full-color photos, HC, 978-1-893361-66-9 **$16.95**

What You Will See Inside a Hindu Temple
by Dr. Mahendra Jani and Dr. Vandana Jani; Full-color photos by Neirah Bhargava and Vijay Dave
8½ x 10½, 32 pp, Full-color photos, HC, 978-1-59473-116-7 **$17.99**

What You Will See Inside a Mosque
by Aisha Karen Khan; Full-color photos by Aaron Pepis
8½ x 10½, 32 pp, Full-color photos, HC, 978-1-893361-60-7 **$16.95**

What You Will See Inside a Synagogue
by Rabbi Lawrence A. Hoffman and Dr. Ron Wolfson; Full-color photos by Bill Aron
8½ x 10½, 32 pp, Full-color photos, HC, 978-1-59473-012-2 **$17.99**

Children's Spirituality

Remembering My Grandparent: A Kid's Own Grief Workbook in the Christian Tradition *by Nechama Liss-Levinson, PhD, and Rev. Molly Phinney Baskette, MDiv* 8 x 10, 48 pp, 2-color text, HC, 978-1-59473-212-6 **$16.99** *For ages 7–13*

Does God Ever Sleep? *by Joan Sauro, CSJ; Full-color photos*
A charming nighttime reminder that God is always present in our lives.
10 x 8½, 32 pp, Quality PB, Full-color photos, 978-1-59473-110-5 **$8.99** *For ages 3–6*

Does God Forgive Me? *by August Gold; Full-color photos by Diane Hardy Waller*
Gently shows how God forgives all that we do if we are truly sorry.
10 x 8½, 32 pp, Quality PB, Full-color photos, 978-1-59473-142-6 **$8.99** *For ages 3–6*

God Said Amen *by Sandy Eisenberg Sasso; Full-color illus. by Avi Katz*
A warm and inspiring tale of two kingdoms that shows us that we need only reach out to each other to find the answers to our prayers.
9 x 12, 32 pp, HC, Full-color illus., 978-1-58023-080-3 **$16.95**
For ages 4 & up (a Jewish Lights book)

How Does God Listen? *by Kay Lindahl; Full-color photos by Cynthia Maloney*
How do we know when God is listening to us? Children will find the answers to these questions as they engage their senses while the story unfolds, learning how God listens in the wind, waves, clouds, hot chocolate, perfume, our tears and our laughter.
10 x 8½, 32 pp, Quality PB, Full-color photos, 978-1-59473-084-9 **$8.99** *For ages 3–6*

In God's Hands *by Lawrence Kushner and Gary Schmidt; Full-color illus. by Matthew J. Baeck*
9 x 12, 32 pp, Full-color illus., HC, 978-1-58023-224-1 **$16.99** *For ages 5 & up (a Jewish Lights book)*

In God's Name *by Sandy Eisenberg Sasso; Full-color illus. by Phoebe Stone*
Like an ancient myth in its poetic text and vibrant illustrations, this award-winning modern fable about the search for God's name celebrates the diversity and, at the same time, the unity of all the people of the world.
9 x 12, 32 pp, HC, Full-color illus., 978-1-879045-26-2 **$16.99**
For ages 4 & up (a Jewish Lights book)

Also available in Spanish: El nombre de Dios
9 x 12, 32 pp, HC, Full-color illus., 978-1-893361-63-8 **$16.95**

In Our Image: God's First Creatures
by Nancy Sohn Swartz; Full-color illus. by Melanie Hall
A playful new twist on the Genesis story—from the perspective of the animals. Celebrates the interconnectedness of nature and the harmony of all living things.
9 x 12, 32 pp, HC, Full-color illus., 978-1-879045-99-6 **$16.95**
For ages 4 & up (a Jewish Lights book)

Noah's Wife: The Story of Naamah
by Sandy Eisenberg Sasso; Full-color illus. by Bethanne Andersen
This new story, based on an ancient text, opens readers' religious imaginations to new ideas about the well-known story of the Flood. When God tells Noah to bring the animals of the world onto the ark, God also calls on Naamah, Noah's wife, to save each plant on Earth.
9 x 12, 32 pp, HC, Full-color illus., 978-1-58023-134-3 **$16.95** *For ages 4 & up (a Jewish Lights book)*

Also available: Naamah: Noah's Wife (A Board Book)
by Sandy Eisenberg Sasso; Full-color illus. by Bethanne Andersen
5 x 5, 24 pp, Board Book, Full-color illus., 978-1-893361-56-0 **$7.99** *For ages 0–4*

Where Does God Live? *by August Gold and Matthew J. Perlman*
Using simple, everyday examples that children can relate to, this colorful book helps young readers develop a personal understanding of God.
10 x 8½, 32 pp, Quality PB, Full-color photo illus., 978-1-893361-39-3 **$8.99** *For ages 3–6*

Spirituality

Next to Godliness: Finding the Sacred in Housekeeping
Edited and with Introductions by Alice Peck
Offers new perspectives on how we can reach out for the Divine.
6 x 9, 224 pp, Quality PB, 978-1-59473-214-0 **$19.99**

Bread, Body, Spirit: Finding the Sacred in Food
Edited and with Introductions by Alice Peck
Explores how food feeds our faith. 6 x 9, 224 pp (est), Quality PB, 978-1-59473-242-3 **$19.99**

Renewal in the Wilderness: A Spiritual Guide to Connecting with God in the Natural World *by John Lionberger*
Reveals the power of experiencing God's presence in many variations of the natural world. 6 x 9, 176 pp, b/w photos, Quality PB, 978-1-59473-219-5 **$16.99**

Honoring Motherhood: Prayers, Ceremonies and Blessings
Edited and with Introductions by Lynn L. Caruso
Journey through the seasons of motherhood. 5 x 7¼, 272 pp, HC, 978-1-59473-239-3 **$19.99**

Soul Fire: Accessing Your Creativity *by Rev. Thomas Ryan, CSP*
Learn to cultivate your creative spirit. 6 x 9, 160 pp, Quality PB, 978-1-59473-243-0 **$16.99**

Technology & Spirituality: How the Information Revolution Affects Our Spiritual Lives *by Stephen K. Spyker* 6 x 9, 176 pp, HC, 978-1-59473-218-8 **$19.99**

Money and the Way of Wisdom: Insights from the Book of Proverbs
by Timothy J. Sandoval, PhD 6 x 9, 192 pp (est), Quality PB, 978-1-59473-245-4 **$16.99**

Awakening the Spirit, Inspiring the Soul
30 Stories of Interspiritual Discovery in the Community of Faiths
Edited by Brother Wayne Teasdale and Martha Howard, MD; Foreword by Joan Borysenko, PhD
6 x 9, 224 pp, HC, 978-1-59473-039-9 **$21.99**

Creating a Spiritual Retirement: A Guide to the Unseen Possibilities in Our Lives
by Molly Srode 6 x 9, 208 pp, b/w photos, Quality PB, 978-1-59473-050-4 **$14.99**
HC, 978-1-893361-75-1 **$19.99**

Finding Hope: Cultivating God's Gift of a Hopeful Spirit
by Marcia Ford 8 x 8, 200 pp, Quality PB, 978-1-59473-211-9 **$16.99**

The Geography of Faith: Underground Conversations on Religious, Political and Social Change *by Daniel Berrigan and Robert Coles* 6 x 9, 224 pp, Quality PB, 978-1-893361-40-9 **$16.95**

Jewish Spirituality: A Brief Introduction for Christians *by Lawrence Kushner*
5½ x 8½, 112 pp, Quality PB, 978-1-58023-150-3 **$12.95** *(a Jewish Lights book)*

Journeys of Simplicity: Traveling Light with Thomas Merton, Bashō, Edward Abbey, Annie Dillard & Others *by Philip Harnden* 5 x 7¼, 144 pp, Quality PB
978-1-59473-181-5 **$12.99** 128 pp, HC, 978-1-893361-76-8 **$16.95**

Keeping Spiritual Balance As We Grow Older: More than 65 Creative Ways to Use Purpose, Prayer, and the Power of Spirit to Build a Meaningful Retirement
by Molly and Bernie Srode 8 x 8, 224 pp, Quality PB, 978-1-59473-042-9 **$16.99**

Spirituality 101: The Indispensable Guide to Keeping—or Finding—Your Spiritual Life on Campus *by Harriet L. Schwartz, with contributions from college students at nearly thirty campuses across the United States* 6 x 9, 272 pp, Quality PB, 978-1-59473-000-9 **$16.99**

Spiritually Incorrect: Finding God in All the Wrong Places *by Dan Wakefield; Illus. by Marian DelVecchio* 5½ x 8½, 192 pp, b/w illus., Quality PB, 978-1-59473-137-2 **$15.99**

Spiritual Manifestos: Visions for Renewed Religious Life in America from Young Spiritual Leaders of Many Faiths *Edited by Niles Elliot Goldstein; Preface by Martin E. Marty*
6 x 9, 256 pp, HC, 978-1-893361-09-6 **$21.95**

A Walk with Four Spiritual Guides: Krishna, Buddha, Jesus, and Ramakrishna
by Andrew Harvey 5½ x 8½, 192 pp, 10 b/w photos & illus., Quality PB, 978-1-59473-138-9 **$15.99**

What Matters: Spiritual Nourishment for Head and Heart
by Frederick Franck 5 x 7¼, 128 pp, 50+ b/w illus., HC, 978-1-59473-013-9 **$16.99**

Who Is My God?, 2nd Edition: An Innovative Guide to Finding Your Spiritual Identity
Created by the Editors at SkyLight Paths 6 x 9, 160 pp, Quality PB, 978-1-59473-014-6 **$15.99**

Spirituality & Crafts

The Knitting Way
A Guide to Spiritual Self-Discovery
by Linda Skolnik and Janice MacDaniels
Examines how you can explore and strengthen your spiritual life through knitting.
7 x 9, 240 pp, Quality PB, b/w photographs, 978-1-59473-079-5 **$16.99**

The Scrapbooking Journey
A Hands-On Guide to Spiritual Discovery
by Cory Richardson-Lauve; Foreword by Stacy Julian
Reveals how this craft can become a practice used to deepen and shape your life.
7 x 9, 176 pp, Quality PB, 8-page full-color insert, plus b/w photographs
978-1-59473-216-4 **$18.99**

The Painting Path
Embodying Spiritual Discovery through Yoga, Brush and Color
by Linda Novick; Foreword by Richard Segalman
Explores the divine connection you can experience through creativity.
7 x 9, 208 pp, 8-page full-color insert, plus b/w photographs
Quality PB, 978-1-59473-226-3 **$18.99**

The Quilting Path
A Guide to Spiritual Discovery through Fabric, Thread and Kabbalah
by Louise Silk
Explores how to cultivate personal growth through quilt making.
7 x 9, 192 pp, Quality PB, b/w photographs and illustrations, 978-1-59473-206-5 **$16.99**

Contemplative Crochet
A Hands-On Guide for Interlocking Faith and Craft
by Cindy Crandall-Frazier; Foreword by Linda Skolnik
Illuminates the spiritual lessons you can learn through crocheting.
7 x 9, 192 pp (est), b/w photographs, Quality PB, 978-1-59473-238-6 **$16.99**

Kabbalah / Enneagram
(from Jewish Lights Publishing)

Awakening to Kabbalah: The Guiding Light of Spiritual Fulfillment
by Rav Michael Laitman, PhD 6 x 9, 192 pp, HC, 978-1-58023-264-7 **$21.99**

Cast in God's Image: Discover Your Personality Type Using the Enneagram and Kabbalah
by Rabbi Howard A. Addison 7 x 9, 176 pp, Quality PB, 978-1-58023-124-4 **$16.95**

Ehyeh: A Kabbalah for Tomorrow *by Dr. Arthur Green*
6 x 9, 224 pp, Quality PB, 978-1-58023-213-5 **$16.99**

The Enneagram and Kabbalah, 2nd Edition: Reading Your Soul
by Rabbi Howard A. Addison 6 x 9, 192 pp, Quality PB, 978-1-58023-229-6 **$16.99**

The Gift of Kabbalah: Discovering the Secrets of Heaven, Renewing Your Life on Earth
by Tamar Frankiel, PhD 6 x 9, 256 pp, Quality PB, 978-1-58023-141-1 **$16.95**
HC, 978-1-58023-108-4 **$21.95**

Kabbalah: A Brief Introduction for Christians
by Tamar Frankiel, PhD 5½ x 8½, 176 pp, Quality PB, 978-1-58023-303-3 **$16.99**

Zohar: Annotated & Explained *Translation and Annotation by Dr. Daniel C. Matt*
Foreword by Andrew Harvey 5½ x 8½, 176 pp, Quality PB, 978-1-893361-51-5 **$15.99**
(a SkyLight Paths book)

Spiritual Practice

Soul Fire: Accessing Your Creativity by Rev. Thomas Ryan, CSP
Shows you how to cultivate your creative spirit as a way to encourage personal growth.
6 x 9, 160 pp, Quality PB, 978-1-59473-243-0 **$16.99**

Running—The Sacred Art: Preparing to Practice
by Dr. Warren A. Kay; Foreword by Kristin Armstrong
Examines how your daily run can enrich your spiritual life.
5½ x 8½, 160 pp, Quality PB, 978-1-59473-227-0 **$16.99**

Hospitality—The Sacred Art: Discovering the Hidden Spiritual Power
of Invitation and Welcome by Rev. Nanette Sawyer; Foreword by Rev. Dirk Ficca
Explores how this ancient spiritual practice can transform your relationships.
5½ x 8½, 192 pp, Quality PB, 978-1-59473-228-7 **$16.99**

Thanking & Blessing—The Sacred Art: Spiritual Vitality through
Gratefulness by Jay Marshall, PhD; Foreword by Philip Gulley
Offers practical tips for uncovering the blessed wonder in our lives—even in trying circumstances. 5½ x 8½, 176 pp, Quality PB, 978-1-59473-231-7 **$16.99**

Everyday Herbs in Spiritual Life: A Guide to Many Practices
by Michael J. Caduto; Foreword by Rosemary Gladstar Explores the power of herbs.
7 x 9, 208 pp, 21 b/w illustrations, Quality PB, 978-1-59473-174-7 **$16.99**

Divining the Body: Reclaim the Holiness of Your Physical Self by Jan Phillips
8 x 8, 256 pp, Quality PB, 978-1-59473-080-1 **$16.99**

Finding Time for the Timeless: Spirituality in the Workweek
by John McQuiston II Simple stories show you how refocus your daily life.
5½ x 6¾, 208 pp, HC, 978-1-59473-035-1 **$17.99**

The Gospel of Thomas: A Guidebook for Spiritual Practice
by Ron Miller; Translations by Stevan Davies
6 x 9, 160 pp, Quality PB, 978-1-59473-047-4 **$14.99**

Earth, Water, Fire, and Air: Essential Ways of Connecting to Spirit
by Cait Johnson 6 x 9, 224 pp, HC, 978-1-893361-65-2 **$19.95**

Labyrinths from the Outside In: Walking to Spiritual Insight—A Beginner's Guide
by Donna Schaper and Carole Ann Camp
6 x 9, 208 pp, b/w illus. and photos, Quality PB, 978-1-893361-18-8 **$16.95**

Practicing the Sacred Art of Listening: A Guide to Enrich Your Relationships
and Kindle Your Spiritual Life—The Listening Center Workshop
by Kay Lindahl 8 x 8, 176 pp, Quality PB, 978-1-893361-85-0 **$16.95**

Releasing the Creative Spirit: Unleash the Creativity in Your Life
by Dan Wakefield 7 x 10, 256 pp, Quality PB, 978-1-893361-36-2 **$16.95**

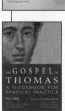

The Sacred Art of Bowing: Preparing to Practice
by Andi Young 5½ x 8½, 128 pp, b/w illus., Quality PB, 978-1-893361-82-9 **$14.95**

The Sacred Art of Chant: Preparing to Practice
by Ana Hernández 5½ x 8½, 192 pp, Quality PB, 978-1-59473-036-8 **$15.99**

The Sacred Art of Fasting: Preparing to Practice
by Thomas Ryan, CSP 5½ x 8½, 192 pp, Quality PB, 978-1-59473-078-8 **$15.99**

The Sacred Art of Forgiveness: Forgiving Ourselves and Others through God's Grace
by Marcia Ford 8 x 8, 176 pp, Quality PB, 978-1-59473-175-4 **$16.99**

The Sacred Art of Listening: Forty Reflections for Cultivating a Spiritual
Practice by Kay Lindahl; Illustrations by Amy Schnapper
8 x 8, 160 pp, b/w illus., Quality PB, 978-1-893361-44-7 **$16.99**

The Sacred Art of Lovingkindness: Preparing to Practice
by Rabbi Rami Shapiro; Foreword by Marcia Ford 5½ x 8½, 176 pp, Quality PB, 978-1-59473-151-8 **$16.99**

Sacred Speech: A Practical Guide for Keeping Spirit in Your Speech
by Rev. Donna Schaper 6 x 9, 176 pp, Quality PB, 978-1-59473-068-9 **$15.99**
HC, 978-1-893361-74-4 **$21.95**

Prayer / Meditation

Sacred Attention: A Spiritual Practice for Finding God in the Moment
by Margaret D. McGee
Framed on the Christian liturgical year, this inspiring guide explores ways to develop a practice of attention as a means of talking—and listening—to God.
6 x 9, 144 pp, HC, 978-1-59473-232-4 **$19.99**

Women Pray: Voices through the Ages, from Many Faiths, Cultures and Traditions
Edited and with Introductions by Monica Furlong
5 x 7¼, 256 pp, Quality PB, 978-1-59473-071-9 **$15.99**

Women of Color Pray: Voices of Strength, Faith, Healing, Hope and Courage *Edited and with Introductions by Christal M. Jackson*
Through these prayers, poetry, lyrics, meditations and affirmations, you will share in the strong and undeniable connection women of color share with God.
5 x 7¼, 208 pp, Quality PB, 978-1-59473-077-1 **$15.99**

Secrets of Prayer: A Multifaith Guide to Creating Personal Prayer in Your Life *by Nancy Corcoran, CSJ*
This compelling, multifaith guidebook offers you companionship and encouragement on the journey to a healthy prayer life. 6 x 9, 160 pp, Quality PB, 978-1-59473-215-7 **$16.99**

Prayers to an Evolutionary God
by William Cleary; Afterword by Diarmuid O'Murchu
Inspired by the spiritual and scientific teachings of Diarmuid O'Murchu and Teilhard de Chardin, reveals that religion and science can be combined to create an expanding view of the universe—an evolutionary faith.
6 x 9, 208 pp, HC, 978-1-59473-006-1 **$21.99**

The Art of Public Prayer: Not for Clergy Only *by Lawrence A. Hoffman*
6 x 9, 288 pp, Quality PB, 978-1-893361-06-5 **$18.99**

A Heart of Stillness: A Complete Guide to Learning the Art of Meditation
by David A. Cooper 5½ x 8½, 272 pp, Quality PB, 978-1-893361-03-4 **$16.95**

Meditation without Gurus: A Guide to the Heart of Practice
by Clark Strand 5½ x 8½, 192 pp, Quality PB, 978-1-893361-93-5 **$16.95**

Praying with Our Hands: 21 Practices of Embodied Prayer from the World's Spiritual Traditions *by Jon M. Sweeney; Photographs by Jennifer J. Wilson; Foreword by Mother Tessa Bielecki; Afterword by Taitetsu Unno, PhD*
8 x 8, 96 pp, 22 duotone photos, Quality PB, 978-1-893361-16-4 **$16.95**

Silence, Simplicity & Solitude: A Complete Guide to Spiritual Retreat at Home
by David A. Cooper 5½ x 8½, 336 pp, Quality PB, 978-1-893361-04-1 **$16.95**

Three Gates to Meditation Practice: A Personal Journey into Sufism, Buddhism, and Judaism *by David A. Cooper* 5½ x 8½, 240 pp, Quality PB, 978-1-893361-22-5 **$16.95**

Prayer / M. Basil Pennington, OCSO

Finding Grace at the Center, 3rd Ed.: The Beginning of Centering Prayer *with Thomas Keating, OCSO, and Thomas E. Clarke, SJ; Foreword by Rev. Cynthia Bourgeault, PhD*
A practical guide to a simple and beautiful form of meditative prayer.
5 x 7¼, 128 pp, Quality PB, 978-1-59473-182-2 **$12.99**

The Monks of Mount Athos: A Western Monk's Extraordinary Spiritual Journey on Eastern Holy Ground *Foreword by Archimandrite Dionysios*
Explores the landscape, the monastic communities, and the food of Athos.
6 x 9, 256 pp, 10+ b/w drawings, Quality PB, 978-1-893361-78-2 **$18.95**

Psalms: A Spiritual Commentary *Illustrations by Phillip Ratner*
Reflections on some of the most beloved passages from the Bible's most widely read book. 6 x 9, 176 pp, 24 full-page b/w illus., Quality PB, 978-1-59473-234-8 **$16.99**
HC, 978-1-59473-141-9 **$19.99**

The Song of Songs: A Spiritual Commentary *Illustrations by Phillip Ratner*
Explore the Bible's most challenging mystical text.
6 x 9, 160 pp, 14 b/w illus., Quality PB, 978-1-59473-235-3 **$16.99**; HC, 978-1-59473-004-7 **$19.99**

About SKYLIGHT PATHS Publishing

SkyLight Paths Publishing is creating a place where people of different spiritual traditions come together for challenge and inspiration, a place where we can help each other understand the mystery that lies at the heart of our existence.

Through spirituality, our religious beliefs are increasingly becoming a part of our lives—rather than *apart* from our lives. While many of us may be more interested than ever in spiritual growth, we may be less firmly planted in traditional religion. Yet, we do want to deepen our relationship to the sacred, to learn from our own as well as from other faith traditions, and to practice in new ways.

SkyLight Paths sees both believers and seekers as a community that increasingly transcends traditional boundaries of religion and denomination—people wanting to learn from each other, *walking together, finding the way.*

For your information and convenience, at the back of this book we have provided a list of other SkyLight Paths books you might find interesting and useful. They cover the following subjects:

Buddhism / Zen	Global Spiritual	Monasticism
Catholicism	Perspectives	Mysticism
Children's Books	Gnosticism	Poetry
Christianity	Hinduism /	Prayer
Comparative	Vedanta	Religious Etiquette
Religion	Inspiration	Retirement
Current Events	Islam / Sufism	Spiritual Biography
Earth-Based	Judaism	Spiritual Direction
Spirituality	Kabbalah	Spirituality
Enneagram	Meditation	Women's Interest
	Midrash Fiction	Worship